⬆ his end up ⬆

his end up

Getting God into the New Theology

VERNARD ELLER

ABINGDON
PRESS
Nashville
New York

HIS END UP

Copyright © 1969 by Abingdon Press

Standard Book Number: 687-17060-5

Library of Congress Catalog Card Number: 69-18452

SET UP, PRINTED, AND BOUND BY THE
PARTHENON PRESS, AT NASHVILLE
TENNESSEE, UNITED STATES OF AMERICA

TO GOD
AND THE PEOPLE,
THE *DRAMATIS PERSONAE*
OF THIS BOOK;
MAY BOTH BE ABLE
TO RECOGNIZE THEMSELVES
HEREIN

CONTENTS

CHAPTER ONE

HOW TO TEETER AS YOU TOTTER

Long experience has demonstrated that teeter-tottering works best when one is willing to let the other fellow have as many up trips as one takes for oneself. And theological-ly speaking, one ought really to let God go up first; it's the only Christian thing to do!

How the new theology might learn this gentle art of the seesaw is the burden of our book. By the new theology, it must be specified, we intend what have been called the "soft radicals" and not the "hard radicals" of the God-is-dead persuasion. It should be quite evident that man cannot teeter-totter alone; if God is dead, the game cannot be the same. In our terms, then, the new theology refers not to any particular school or system but to that contemporary style of Christian thought which is marked by its use of such Bonhoefferian slogans as "turning to the world," "religionless Christianity," "man come of age," "as though God did not exist," "the man for others," "secularization."

It is not our desire to speak *about* this new theology; enough of that has been done already. Neither would we want to be understood as speaking *against* it. Our intent is to speak *from* it, *with* it, but also *to* it.

The genealogy of the new theologians—if we disregard the numerous philosophers, artists, and social scientists who also have had a hand in things—is rather easy to trace. (Lay readers will have to forgive and overlook the name-dropping in which we are about to indulge, but we are leading up to a point which should be just as pertinent for those who are not acquainted with these theologians as for those who are.)

Without question, the father is Dietrich Bonhoeffer—whether the sons be prodigal or otherwise. Barth and Brunner are the grandfathers, with Buber as an uncle and Tillich and Bultmann no more than friends (?) of the family. The great-grandfathers are Kierkegaard and the two Blumhardts, J. C. and his son Christoph, the latter being forgotten ancestors but ones whose credentials have been carefully checked out.[1]

The family history, although an exciting story in its own right, also reveals a rather distressing development: succeeding generations are losing both their interest and proficiency in the old family sport of teeter-tottering.

Intellectuals prefer to call the game "dialectics," but by whatever name, Grandfathers Kierkegaard and Blumhardt were world champions. Kierkegaard was the virtuoso; "dialectic" was the self-conscious method by which he made his reputation. He understood that any theological truth has two ends and that the only way to hold both in view is to keep the teeter tottering. Kierkegaard's dialectic, therefore, is most dynamic in character—something quite different from the Hegelian trick which gets both ends up by breaking the board in the middle and leaning the two pieces together into a synthesis. Hegel's may be dialectic, but it is no good way to play seesaw.

The two ends (poles) of a Kierkegaardian dialectic are not contradictory concepts, nor is the one the negative obverse of the other. Each is a true idea, and ultimately they are found to be complementary. In fact, the whole truth of either is found only as the two are kept in relationship. Nevertheless, the two concepts are different enough that their compatibility

[1] Gerhard Sauter, *Die Theologie des Reiches Gottes beim aelteren und juengeren Blumhardt* (1962).

11

is not immediately evident. But Kierkegaard meets the question, "How can they both be true?" not as many contemporary dialectitians do, with the ambiguous shrug, "They just are!" Rather, his is the effort to delineate the relationship, to show that they are indeed two ends of the same board, and to establish the relationship so solidly that neither one of the concepts can be considered without involving the other.

In doing this, Kierkegaard's theological movement is actually quite akin to that of a teeter-totter. The principle is "balanced imbalance." When a teeter board is in simple, static balance, both players are hung up in midair. When it is a case of simple imbalance, the heavy man is stuck hard aground while the light man is just as immobilized high asky. Seesawing takes place only when the imbalance toward one end immediately creates the condition for its counter movement, an imbalance toward the other end. The movement must be self-perpetuating. And thus, because Kierkegaardian dialectic *is* movement, a movement of thought, any effort to resolve (or divorce) the polarities, achieve static balance, or find a synthesis, is to kill the dialectic, not consummate it.

If Kierkegaard was the virtuoso, the recognized champion of dialectical teetering, the Blumhardts would seem to have been rank amateurs. They never discussed the theory of the game and were not even aware that they were playing it. Yet they were among the best. They got that way simply by imitating the movements of the Bible—which is where seesaw theology was invented and which ultimately was the source of Kierkegaard's elegant theophilosophizing as well as the Blumhardts' simple pastoring. Within the grand context of the balanced imbalance between God's role and man's role in the world, the Bible handles such specific dialectics as grace and law, universalism and particularism, election and responsibility, faith and works, lordship and servanthood. In all these the Bible, unlike much of subsequent theologizing, strives for true dialectical "movement" rather than a synthesizing "solution."

The basic achievement of the Blumhardtian dialectic, then, was to portray the dynamic reality of the kingdom of God in such a way that it clearly is *God's* reign and yet presently effective in this world, in the lives of real people, and with man having a significant and active role. And although the Blumhardts did it intuitively and with no self-consciousness at all, a most competent job of teeter-tottering was the only way of doing justice to their subject matter.

As descendants of both Kierkegaard and Blumhardt, Barth and Brunner inherited a feel for the teeter-totter, and theirs, indeed, was known as "dialectical theology"—although there is evidence that Barth really got the hang of the game comparatively late, with his *The Humanity of God,* a seesaw title if ever there was one.

But in the next generation, with Bonhoeffer, appeared a new technique—what might be called "the delayed teeter." It had been as much as a matter of conscience with Kierkegaard never to discuss one pole of a dialectic without calling attention to the other as well; the two were to be kept in conscious relationship. But although Bonhoeffer undeniably was a good man on the seesaw, he tended to operate with such a long board that it sometimes is difficult to see what he is about. By reading far enough in Bonhoeffer one usually can find a right-hand concept to balance up the left-hand emphasis of the moment; but Bonhoeffer's tendency was to come down hard on one end at a time, without making it explicit that his movement was in fact a dialectical one. At points, indeed, one must use the "early" Bonhoeffer to balance off against the "late" Bonhoeffer—although there is evidence enough to indicate that actually there was only one, the dialectical Bonhoeffer, rather than two, sequential Bonhoeffers.

It is easy to see, then, how it should happen that in the current generation the new theologians might "creatively misuse" Bonhoeffer so as to lose the art of the seesaw altogether. In particular there has been a failure to do theology so that emphasis upon God's role is put into dynamic alternation with man's. The God-is-dead men, of course, have gone so far as to saw off God's end of the board, but even the "soft radicals" aren't doing too well at giving God his share of the upswings. What they have done is to latch onto the themes of their fathers (notably Bonhoeffer) in which the upswings of man are accentuated and overlook the counter movements that bring God's end up. Kierkegaard, interestingly enough, has been "creatively misused" both ways: Barth read Kierkegaard and found "the infinite qualitative distinction between God and man"; Bultmann read him and found the cruciality of man's existential decision.

The thesis of this book, then, is that the new theologians would do well to take another look at their forefathers—not this time to garner more slogans for creative misusing but to learn the fine old game of teeter-tottering. It is not that the new theology must be rejected; it does desperately need some balancing up. It takes two for the seesaw, and modern theology must discover how to give God his due.

However, it must be clearly understood that nowhere in this book are we suggesting that the actual life relationship between man and God should be described as a teeter-totter. Far be it from us to imply that that relationship is one of parity, that man carries weight comparable to God's. We are talking only about "theologizing," only about how men should relate their *thoughts about man* to their *thoughts about God* and not about their own faith relationship *to* God. Much of classical theology spoke after the pattern: God-God-God-God-man. Much of contemporary theology speaks: man-man-man-

man-God. We are proposing simply that the most accurate pattern for theology is: God-man-God-man-God-man—which, we submit, is the pattern of the Bible itself.

What follows does not pretend to be itself a balanced theology. Rather than being a performance on the teeter-totter, it is an ephemeral word on how to. And because there is no reason to try to improve on what others are saying about the upswings of man, the concentration here shall be on up-swinging God. This book is intended as an addition to the new theology and not a replacement for it. To borrow a phrase from the old master, it is presented as a "corrective."

CHAPTER TWO

ALL THE WORLD'S A STAGE—THEOLOGICALLY SPEAKING

Shakespeare said it but was not speaking theologically. Bonhoeffer did not say it, but he was speaking theologically. We need only get the two together.

Perhaps the most basic question to which the new theology should address itself is: Does man need God or doesn't he? In some ways this is prior even to the question of God's existence. Unless God is needed, his existence is beside the point, an academic question and meaningless affirmation. Yet, of late, there has been a great deal of wobbling on this matter.

Bonhoeffer can be and is quoted as though man does not need God: "man has come of age," "we must live as though God did not exist," "we can no longer be religious men." The God-is-dead men have drawn the clear and consistent conclusion; and certainly it is to be taken for granted that their proposition has more to do with man's need for God than anything concerning God himself. But even the soft radicals, although refusing to deny God's existence, have failed almost entirely to assign a function to that existence—to say *why* man should be interested in whether God is dead or alive. Does man need God or does he not? If so, wherein and for what purposes? It is to these questions that modern theology is either going to have to put up or shut up.

If one reads dialectically, Bonhoeffer is found to provide some teeter to go along with the totter that the new theologians have read out of him. I don't know whether it has been noticed before, but Bonhoeffer had a thing about "the middle." At various points in his writings he has "man in the middle," "the tree of life and the tree of the knowledge of good and evil in the middle," "God in the middle," "Christ the center." Apparently he wanted to direct his theological show so as to have the whole cast massed in center stage. But the key to all this symbolism is in making the subtle but crucial distinction between "the center" and "the middle." We shall get to the "centrality" of God in due course, but the need for God comes about precisely because man is in "the middle."

The picture is this: "All the world's a stage, and all the men and women merely players"—in what appears to be a drama of some sort. But that is just the problem! Man is plunked down in the middle—right in the middle of Act II (or Act XXII)—and *he doesn't have a script!* Man is stuck in the middle, and he doesn't have the wherewithal to get out and up to a perspective from which he can see what the whole business is about and where it is headed. Obviously the experience of no one individual is sufficient to make sense of the whole; and as regards the total sweep of human existence and history, even the sum of man's wisdom hardly constitutes a playwright's achievement. Although it may be that modern man is sufficiently "of age" that he can survive and keep a show on the boards—shift the scenery, run the lights, and put on quite a song and dance—this does not mean that he necessarily is playing the role or furthering the drama that the theater was built to house.

But perhaps what we are in is not a drama but a happening or improvisation! Precisely, and that is the question, the question upon which all others—including "To be or not to be?"—depend. Much of the new theology seems to be building upon the "happening" premise. Man (both individually and collectively) is to write his own script as well as play the role. He is to improvise as he goes along, do as the spirit (his own spirit) leads him, and evaluate the result by how he "feels" about it. Although the construction of the stage and the presence of other players impose some limits, man himself is to be the norm and judge of his own actions. This is the nature of a happening.

And yet if there is one affirmation that is basic to the Bible from Genesis to Revelation (Ecclesiastes only excepted), it is that what is being played out on the stage of this world is a drama and in no sense a happening. Let a man pronounce God dead as often as he likes, if he still sees history as a drama he has not lost contact with the biblical God. But let him say, "Lord, Lord," and recite the most orthodox of creeds, if he sees history as a happening he has cut himself off from any claim to the name "Christian." Would that the divide might be made here rather than over the hypothetical question as to whether God is dead or alive. If history is seen as a drama, then God will come alive, for a drama necessarily brings with it a need—the need for a playwright.

Man in the middle is man in a muddle. Although, in one sense, he does not need the Playwright in order *to be,* he does in order to know *who* he is to be. He does not so much require the Playwright to tell him his next line, signal him when to stand, sit, cross, or exit—competent actors could pretty well figure out these things for themselves. But where the help of the Playwright is an absolute "must" is in assigning the actors their roles—defining who they are, how each fits into the general action that is to transpire, and where this overall action is to come out.

Bonhoeffer put man in the middle, but it was Kierkegaard who first portrayed man as playing a role before God the Playwright. And quite apart from that potent parable, Kierkegaard also was the one who saw God as the source of every man's identification: "There is only One who knows what He Himself is, that is God; and He knows also what every man in himself is, for it is precisely by being before God that every man is. The man who is not before God is not himself, for this a man can be only by being before Him who is in and for Himself. If one is oneself by being in Him who is in and for Himself, one can be in others and before others, but one cannot by being merely before others be oneself." [1]

If existence is a drama in which we are actors, then man *needs* the word of the Playwright to tell him what a man is; and more specifically, Vernard Eller needs the Playwright to tell him who is this Vernard Eller character he is supposed to be playing.

The reason neither Vernard Eller nor mankind as a whole has the ghost of a chance of figuring out the plot line and

[1] "The Anxiety of Lowliness" (Part I, Discourse 3) in *Christian Discourses,* trans. Walter Lowrie (New York: Oxford University Press, 1939), p. 43.

21

his own role simply by looking around from his spot in the middle is that he does not have access to the two most critical parts of any play, namely, the beginning and the end. The play itself is bigger than any and all of the actors. Man's need of God, then, is precisely concomitant with the fact that he is in the middle.

The opening scene of a play is important, but it is the end, the finis, that is all-controlling. Every true drama is "eschatological" (end-state oriented) in that how it "comes out" determines whether the whole effort was worthwhile. Yet, apart from the end itself, the beginning is the most eschatological moment of a play. It is in the opening scene, for instance, we discover that there is a murder which will need to be solved and are presented the facts of the case within which the solution must come. The final scene, then, brings that solution and the apprehension of the butler. But the middle—the middle is precisely that portion of the play which is most confusing and in which the plot line is least "guessable."

If the world is a stage on which a cosmological drama is being played, then history must be eschatological in the same sense a ball game is. Consider that the very concept "ball game" is made possible only by the rule that declares that at some point it is "all over." An unending contest would not be a game but simply fooling around. And every action of a true ball game exists for the sake of and derives its meaning from the *final* score. A given hit cannot be said to have brought in the *winning* run, nor a given out to have *saved* the game, except as an eschatological observation made from the standpoint of the game's end. To be ahead ten to one in the sixth inning is of no significance whatever except as it contributes to being ahead *at the end*.

Just so with true drama. No sequence of action is meaningful until one knows how it comes out; and "how it comes out" can be determined only after the sequence has been declared ended. Without eschatological perspective the only meaning the drama of history can be made to render is that of a happening, namely, the momentary satisfaction that comes in the course of doing the doing. This is why the Theater of the Absurd ultimately is unsatisfying and not strictly deserving of the name "drama"; the action opens at random and closes, not with a "final curtain," but with either the playwright's or the playgoer's desire to go home. Such theater justifies itself as being a reflection of life—and thus is itself blasphemy, if the Christian contention is correct that life is a drama and not a happening.

The eschatological nature of drama is most important to our analogy. It suggests that world history also is eschatological and that, because man is confined to the middle and thus prevented from being his own eschatologist, he must turn to the Playwright who does have an eschatological perspective.

And this precisely is the role which the Bible consistently assigns to God. It is only through God the Alpha that man has access to the eschatological beginning and through God the Omega that he has access to the eschatological denouement. It is only from such an eschatological perspective that he can know Jesus as the Christ, for "Christ" is nothing more nor less than an eschatological concept dealing with how the world is to come out.

The Blumhardtian contribution to theology comes in just at this point. It is a version of Christian thought that speaks consistently from the eschatological perspective *which is the kingdom of God*. It proposes that all history—including my personal history—is controlled from and pointed toward this end. It is a theology oriented toward the future, a theology of promise and hope—these being the New Testament equivalent of "Christian eschatological perspective." Bonhoeffer may even have been reflecting a Blumhardtian influence when, in direct connection with locating man in the middle, he observed that "the church speaks from the end of all things."

That which man needs and needs unconditionally, if he is to have any chance of fulfilling his role in the drama which is history, is a script, or an eschatological perspective (which, in the final analysis, is what a script is). It is this that his being confined to the middle absolutely prohibits him from invent-

24

ing for himself. And so it is this that comprises his absolute
need for God.

But Bonhoeffer is quoted to the effect that man does not
need God! Yes, that is the other end of his teeter board, the
one to which the new theology already has given considerable
attention but of which we dare not lose sight just because
we are concentrating on how to teeter rather than totter.

The God man does not need, Bonhoeffer says, is *deus ex
machina*. We are grateful that Bonhoeffer chose a theatrical
metaphor and so enabled us to maintain the theme of this
chapter. *Deus ex machina,* the god of the machine, is an
emergency device used by incompetent playwrights. A poor
writer has a way of getting his characters involved in situations
that are so complicated and desperate that there is no possibility of finding a solution within the context of the situation
itself. At such a juncture the playwrighting hack, in a frantic
effort to make things come out "right," is forced to introduce
a *deus ex machina*. In some old plays this took the form of
an entrance by a god, angel, fairy, or some such—perhaps
actually lowered from the flies via celestial machinery. But the
same principle is involved whenever, out of desperation, a
playwright, late in the day, imports into the plot an essentially
foreign character or action, the sole purpose of which is to

rescue a situation that the author can no longer control out of the resources of the plot itself.

But God is not an incompetent Playwright, and Bonhoeffer was not accusing him of such. Who is, then? Man in the middle is. As long as man tries to be his own playwright, provide his own eschatological script, he continually writes himself into a corner; things just will not come out right. In this predicament religious man always is inclined to take the way of the hack and ring in a *deus ex machina*. But this is a role that God, the God of the Bible, consistently refuses to play. If he is to be truly God, it must be as God the Playwright, God at the center, and not as a stopgap to cover for man's incompetency, the butler who is introduced in the final scene to take the rap for a murder the playwright himself couldn't handle.

Thus, in the final analysis, Bonhoeffer was making the same point when he said that man does not need God as he was when saying that man does need God—which, incidentally, is the only way to teeter-totter. Man does not need to resort to a *deus ex machina*. And why not? Not because he can write better plays than that, but because there is a Playwright who already has done a script which entirely avoids the need for a *deus ex machina*. The very fact that man gets in the spot where he needs a *deus ex machina* is proof that he needs God—God the Playwright. And as soon as man is willing to accept his script from God the Playwright, he loses all need for a *deus ex machina*. Precisely the reason man does not need God in the one role is that he has cast him in the other. It is as simple as that.

Although we have not yet said all that must be said about man's need for God, we have perhaps said as much as our drama analogy will support. Let us try another tack.

CHAPTER THREE

ALL THE WORLD'S
A JUNGLE, TOO

Neither Shakespeare nor Bonhoeffer said this, but some-
body must have. In any case, we still are speaking theologically.

"All the world's a stage" was an analogy taking its cue
from the Bonhoefferian dictum "man in the middle." "All
the world's a jungle" is an analogy building upon the Bonhoefferian dictum "God in the center." Yet both analogies
speak to the same point and elucidate the same relationship
between God and man. The crucial distinction is between
"the middle" in the first phrase and "the center" in the

second; they are not interchangeable. It would not be correct to say that God is in the middle, for as we have expounded the matter, his Godness resides precisely in the fact that his perspective is eschatological, encompassing beginning, middle, and end. Neither would it be correct to say that man is in the center, for reasons we shall consider now.

One implication of our previous analogy was that the playwright's essential function is to provide orientation for the actors, that God is the orienter of man. The same idea is central in our new analogy. All the world's a jungle, and all the men and women wanderers in it. But in the center of this jungle stands an orientation point, a beacon. Picture it as you will: a light on a tower, a horn, a radio or radar transmitter. In any case, this is God in the center.

But consider if you will that the presence and use of this beacon spells precisely the difference between an explorer and the fellow who is simply lost in the jungle—and some difference that! An explorer is such and his journeyings meaningful and contributive only because he keeps himself located in relation to some base point. It is because he knows where he is (in relation to the beacon) that he can tell where he has been and where he is going. The man who is lost, on the other hand, by virtue of the very fact that he has broken contact with the beacon, knows not where he has been, where he is, or where he is going. An explorer can see the terrain and relate himself to it; little boy lost sees only trees—and they all look alike. It is the presence of God in the center that makes the world itself come clear; it is God's orienting function that makes a turn to the world possible, for certainly it is the explorer and not the floundering wanderer who can be said to have turned to the world in any significant sense.

On the stage the Playwright tells the actor *who* he is, and in the jungle the Beacon tells the explorer *where* he is, but at base these both come to the same thing. To know *who* I am is nothing more than to know *where* I stand in the nexus of relationships in which I find myself; and once I know *who* I am, I have solved the problem as to where and how to take my stand. But either way, man's need is for God in the center, for a God who will be the Centerer—a script that reveals something of the wherefrom, wherefore, and whereto of the drama that is human existence; a beacon that stands high enough above the jungle that it organizes that jungle into a landscape. Man needs a point of orientation.

But Bonhoeffer said that man does not need God! True; so prepare to totter. Consider that, apart from beacons, there is another method of handling men in jungles: build a stockade to keep the jungle out and the men in. Very good; and this is precisely how religious man has been inclined to use God. Obviously, God the Stockade is not God the Center, but

30

God the Perimeter. This God affords security and protection; but just as *deus ex machina* was a desperate measure to save an incompetent playwright, so is God the Stockade a desperate measure to save a cowardly explorer. But it won't do. Man was never intended to be a playwright, and God—the God of the Bible—is not about to cover for him when he makes a mess of it. And man *was* intended to be an explorer, and God—the God of the Bible—is not about to fence out the jungle when man gets scared of it.

The difference between our two analogies is significant. Modern man, the vaunted man of the twentieth century, does very much fancy himself as something of a playwright, as author of his own script; and to this extent he is completely wrongheaded in his efforts. But as regards the jungle, modern man has declared in no uncertain terms that he ain't afraid of nothing. Tear down the stockade; here comes a real, big-as-life explorer! Man has come of age! Bonhoeffer said it; Bonhoeffer meant it; and Bonhoeffer is right. But what Bonhoeffer neither said nor meant was that man is thereby saved or that just because God the Stockade is no longer needed or wanted, God is no longer needed—period.

Man's new stance toward the jungle of the world does indeed mark an advance (better, the possibility of an advance). As Bonhoeffer pointed out, the history of the Christian centuries is this: Earlier men, because of their scientific ignorance, tended to keep the stockade perimeter small and leave to God the management of all the mysteries of the jungle which man himself could not explain or comprehend. But particularly through the progress of science and technology man discovered that there was more and more of the jungle which he could map and manage on his own. God's perimeter was being pushed back and back, no matter how much religious men protested. God had to go—if indeed it were the case that the stockade truly was God rather than a religious misunderstanding of God. And now the stockade is down; man has come of age; no one dares presume to lay down boundaries beyond which man cannot explore—that ploy has failed every time it has been tried.

The stockade is down, but (note carefully) this does not automatically constitute man as an explorer. The poor fellow lost in the jungle is also without a stockade. So the destruction of the stockade only opens the *possibility* of man's becoming an explorer—if he is willing to recognize God the Beacon. The situation boils down to this: Man's coming of age, his outgrowing the need for God the Perimeter, makes all the more imperative his need for God the Center. Indeed, the farther out he goes, the more critical becomes his need for sightings of the base point. The man who even now is out far enough to control space and the power of the atom and who soon may control the secret of life itself—he jolly well better find out who he

32

is and where he stands before he is swallowed up by the very jungle he thinks he is exploring.

But conversely, once a man gets a line on the center and orients himself to it, then in very truth there is no limit to how far he can go. Then—but only then—is he free to become the explorer which he wants to be and which God has wanted him to be from the beginning. Then the world is his— as God intended it should be. This is the good news—the gospel that Blumhardt and Bonhoeffer proclaim—and emphatically not the bare announcement that man has come of age and thrown down the stockade.

The case is similar as regards Bonhoeffer's word that we must live as though God did not exist. This is no denigration of God but a hymn in his honor. Consider that the old Stockade God was a very obvious and conspicuous God. Every way man turned he faced him—bumped into him in fact, whether as a limiting imposition or as the wall beneath which one crouched. In either case, both Christians and onlookers knew that here was a God of blatant and self-evident sovereignty.

But on the other hand, consider God the Beacon. His position is behind man rather than always set before his face. To an onlooker it might seem as though the dependency were less close than it had been before, as though perhaps God did not even exist. But the explorer himself knows better, knows that he needs God all the more, precisely because the relationship is not as self-evident as it had been, because it has become "an arcane discipline," so to speak. Yet the explorer knows that he can explore only as long as he maintains communication with the center; there are no stockade walls to bump him into remembrance.

And God's sovereignty? Tell me, which man exercises the truest sovereignty over the circus lion: the roustabout who handles him with chutes, prods, and ropes, or the trainer who manages the beast's performance with a word of command? And which is the sovereignty worthy of God: the sovereignty of the perimeter or that of the center? An explorer is a trained man.

Nevertheless, have it as you will, call him Playwright or call him Beacon, God's role constitutes a limit on man's freedom—which is precisely what arouses trepidations within the new theology and new morality. Very true; and yet it was Bonhoeffer himself who spoke of God as being man's "limit." The crux of the matter comes, however, with the dialectic that obtains between limit and freedom; the two do not necessarily stand as mutually exclusive.

Certainly it is a limitation—perhaps even a humiliating one —to have to go to the playwright for one's script; but the actor who is plunked down upon the stage in the middle of Act II, is he a *free* man? He would hardly describe the experience so. Rather, it is upon getting hold of a script that he

34

becomes free, free to be the actor he is, free to play the role that is his.

Certainly it is a limitation—perhaps even a humiliating one —for the explorer continually to have to stop and take sight on the beacon; but is the explorer who has no beacon a *free* man? A man lost in the jungle hardly would describe his situation so. No, it is nothing else than his tie to the beacon that makes the explorer free for his explorations. And this suggests a little different concept of "limit," the one Bonhoeffer discusses specifically.

That *God* is the Center means that *man* dare not try to be. God is not a limiting perimeter that fences man in; he is a limit close around the center to keep man out. Man should love that limit which is precisely the source and guarantee of his freedom. But observe what happens when he does not. Man, vain creature that he is, wants to be *really* free and so be both explorer and beacon all at once. He wants to carry his own bench mark with him, wear his beacon on his hat, as it were—thus making it easier to keep track of. This makes sense—about as much sense as the fellow in the Little Moron joke who, in order to mark a special fishing spot so that he could come back the next day, painted an X on the side of his boat. Obviously a wandering beacon is no beacon at all and, rather than creating freedom, creates nothing but chaos.

No, the Center must be inviolate; that spot must be God's

and only God's if man is to have any freedom at all. Certainly not every limit, but at least this one is in all truth the source of, rather than a threat to, human freedom. And yet man, vain creature that he is, just cannot bring himself to accept the fact.

There is more that needs to be said about man's freedom and God's, but at this point our analogy has reached *its* limit; we will have to go to another. Our analogies also have failed us in another way. God either as Playwright or as Beacon suggests something too impersonal to do justice to the case; so let us take care of that little matter before returning to an investigation of freedom. But our argument thus far has been that, to the question, "Does man need God or doesn't he?" the new theology could answer with a much more emphatic yes than thus far has been forthcoming.

CHAPTER FOUR

IT HAS TO BE YOU;
NONE OTHER WILL DO

Given man's need for God as we have assessed it, what sort of God will it take to fill the bill?

Strangely enough, this marks a somewhat rare approach to the problem of God for modern theology. Those contemporary theologians who speak of God at all seem more often to take as their starting point: "Any God will do as long as he can bear the name; our interest is simply to establish the existence of something that might be called 'God.' Whether he can handle the functions that the Christian gospel assigns to him is not our concern. Our concern is to draw a picture that modern man will buy; can we explicate a God that our contemporaries will approve?"

If I may say so, this approach is slightly wacky—like trying to measure Mt. Rainier so that it will come out at the height most convenient for mountain climbers. In fact, there is something atheistic about the whole procedure—as if the theologian's job were to invent God rather than discover him. But undoubtedly what has skewed the endeavor is the assumption that the big hang-up which keeps modern man from accepting Christianity is an intellectual one. If only we could come up with a concept of God that would not offend the sophisticated intellectuality of modern thinkers, then, it is assumed, they would be ready and eager to join up.

Kierkegaard saw through this fallacy more than a hundred years ago: "People try to persuade us that the objections against Christianity spring from doubt. That is a complete misunderstanding. The objections against Christianity spring from insubordination, the dislike of obedience, rebellion against all authority. As a result people have hitherto been beating the air in their struggle against objections, because they have fought intellectually with doubt instead of fighting morally with rebellion." [1]

Kierkegaard gets to the heart of the matter, for although

[1] Papirer VIII¹A6 quoted in the Translators' Introduction to Kierkegaard's *Works of Love,* trans. Howard and Edna Hong (New York: Harper & Row, 1962), p. 9.

the avowed goal of the theologians is to make the idea of God more readily understandable, their efforts have the reverse effect. It is getting to the place that one must have a doctorate in philosophy with a major in Heidegger, Whitehead, or some such technician before one is competent to understand current explanations of who God is. If this is the way modern man is going to come to know God, God help modern man—and God help God!

The consideration that makes all these intellectual gymnastics necessary is the attempt to come up with a God who is not "supernatural," it being this aspect of the matter that modern man cannot be expected to swallow. But if the old supernatural God has been found too much to accept, the new unsupernatural God is proving too much to understand. And the question even then remains as to whether he is God enough to do the job.

It should be said that none of the fathers of the new theology (neither Bonhoeffer, Barth, Brunner, Buber, Blumhardt, nor Kierkegaard) saw any problem with the old God or made any effort to de-supernaturalize him. That concern has been imported into the new theology out of an alien, philosophically oriented tradition. Notice, for example, how J. A. T. Robinson, the eclectic new theologian of *Honest to God* fame, took his doctrine of God directly from Tillich and Bultmann and then used it to expound Bonhoeffer in a completely distorted way.

Whether two such diverse traditions can be forced to speak the same language is very problematic, to say the least.

Part of the difficulty comes through the fact that the word "supernatural" is as slippery as any in circulation; there is no agreement on what it means. If calling God supernatural has to mean that he is remote and detached from this world, then neither the Bible nor any significant segment of modern theology has held for a supernatural God; that battle is a fake one. If calling God supernatural means that one has to posit as his locus another world over against this one, a "spiritual" realm distinct and divorced from the one in which we live our everyday lives, then again the battle is a fake one; neither Bonhoeffer nor any other responsible theologian would be inclined to argue the point.

No, if the issue to be treated is real, then the de-supernaturalized God must be one who can be defined exhaustively out of the same nexus of items and events that we use in understanding all other phenomena of this life and world. God must be identified as an item, an aspect, a dimension of human experience wholly amenable to the same approaches and methodologies man uses with regard to the rest of his experiences. A supernatural God, on the other hand, is one who cannot be defined without going outside and beyond the normal categories by which man explains the world. Either God must be thought of as lying totally within what we know as "this world" or else as being too big to fit that circumference: this is the issue at stake.

Within such a frame of reference it must be clear that the *function* of God as we have outlined it in previous chapters as much as demands that God be supernatural. And if our understanding of Bonhoeffer and predecessors is correct, their thought too as much as demands a supernatural God. The very quality of the playwright upon which we were intent was that he can instruct the actors only because he speaks from a perspective that is larger than the play itself. Confined as they are to the middle, the actors can see the play only from within; but although still quite capable of acting within the play, the playwright is the one who, by definition, can get above and beyond to the point from which it can be seen as a whole. The playwright, even while active in the play, is categorically and unconditionally different from all that makes up the play itself.

Just so, the beacon must be wholly other than jungle. It is true that the beacon also must be *in the jungle*—and to call God supernatural does not in any sense imply or necessitate his removal *from the world*. All the Bonhoefferian emphases about God's being in and identifying with the world can be maintained just as well with a supernatural God as with a naturalized one; there is no justification for reading Bonhoeffer as though he pointed toward a de-supernaturalized God. The beacon must be *in* the jungle if it is to serve the men who are there, but it cannot be *of* the jungle if it is to be a beacon; it must represent a more-than-jungle perspective. By definition, an orientation point is one introduced into a system from outside, in relation to which the system can then be organized; if it grows out of the system it hardly qualifies as *orientation*.

So as the playwright must be "super-play" and the beacon "super-jungle," so must God be "super-natural"; and that simplifies our definition tremendously. No longer need we try to construct an optical illusion (theological doctrine) in which some aspect of a system appears to be bigger than the system itself.

God is *a person*. This, we will contend, is the only sort of God who has a chance of fulfilling the God-need of man. And when we call God "a person" we mean to be speaking literally; our intention is to come to a definition of "a person" which can be applied with equal accuracy either to God or to a man. Modern theology needs to be forced to speak of God *literally;* any other sort of language too easily can become a mere juggling of words. And unless something literal can be said about God it will be next to impossible to convince anyone that he is for real.

Up to this point we have spoken a great deal by way of analogy—and we shall continue to do so. Neither do we deny that it is by drawing analogies from the human person that

42

we come to understand the God person. But analogy dare not become—and we will attempt not to use it as—an escape from speaking literally. Indeed, an analogy should be a means of becoming more and more literal. Any analogy is of value only as the speaker makes abundantly clear which points of his comparison are intended as direct equation. A table can be taken as a valid analogue of a horse only when it is specified that each has four legs and when "leg" is defined in such a way that it is as literally true of the one as of the other. Any true analogy must proceed from an identifiable point of literal equation; all other sorts are but equivocation. And God as a person is what we intend as our literal starting point.

But to call God a person immediately creates difficulties both for laymen and the professionals. The layman's hang-up is that he is not used to thinking of "a person" without thinking of "a body," substance, a spatio-temporal locus. In such terms, then, to call God a person is to localize him in time and space, which in turn is to put him, with us human persons, into the middle—and thus he is robbed of his function as orientation point. The other possibility is to give him another order of time and space (if such there be), to locate him some-*where* else, in a spatio-temporal continuum existing above and independent of ours. The difficulty, of course, is that there is no evidence of a "somewhere" other than here, of a second world hanging outside ours. And even if there were, this would have the inevitable effect of divorcing God from our world, at least to the extent of locating his "home" elsewhere.

Our plan is to get around these difficulties by showing that the concept "a person" does not necessarily involve a substantial body, does not commit itself to the necessity of a point location. We need simply to think in somewhat deeper terms about what it means to be "a person."

The hang-up of the professional is a little different. For one thing, to call God "a person" immediately is to speak of a supernatural God. If "embodied" human beings are taken as the norm for "natural" person, then a radically different form of personhood must be accounted *super*natural. Yet obviously it is not our intention to do anything about this objection, seeing that we have established God's supernaturalness as being the first requirement for his fulfilling the role of God. Any theologian who has a prejudice against the supernatural is going to have to get over that one without our help.

Another problem for the professional comes about in that calling God a person immediately puts him into a class with the other persons who are human beings. God then becomes an entity among other entities; and it is possible to think of a greater, larger God, namely, one who in himself constitutes a class which subsumes all other classes. But here too the philosophers have created the problem for themselves—and not without considerable effort. Neither the Bible nor Chris-

44

tian thought in general has required that God be equated with the biggest thought that can be thunk; that is the sort of bigness that impresses only philosophers and about which real people (and real Gods) couldn't care less. Besides, start down that road and there is no end. God is Being Itself. That is pretty big, but it can be topped. God is the Ground of Being. But why stop there? I can think of the Ground of the Ground of Being (or the Bedrock of the Ground of Being) if I scrunch my brain hard enough.

The Bible pictures God in his omnipotence as being the greatest power among other, non-God powers—but certainly not as the summating encompassment of all power. His omnipresence means that he is more mobile than most—not that he is the presence of everything that is present. As a person, God is the greatest—but not by that token the personhood of humanity *en masse*. There is no commonsense reason why God should not be one entity among other entities. In this regard we are not inclined to demand more of God than does the Bible itself. It may well be that your God is too small, but it also is possible to emasculate God by making him too big. Get God too large, and there is nothing that even can be said *about* him, let alone *to* him or in converse *with* him. This problem too we must leave for the professionals to solve for themselves.

Very well then; to call God "a person" is not the thing to

do. But we sin boldly: God is a person. But what, pray tell, is "a person"?

A person is an identifiable pattern of actions. Before we get through, we likely will have modified this definition beyond all recognition, but it is a place to start. "Pattern" itself is probably not the right word, but it will have to do until someone proposes a better. If "pattern" suggests a snowflake-type drawing from the last chapter of a geometry book, this is something much too regular, symmetrical, and formal to suit our intentions. And if "pattern" suggests a template, this is something much too fixed and determined. A little later we will speak of pattern as "melody"; but consider here that a melody is a pattern of notes of such flexibility and "life" that it can be greatly varied as to tempo, pitch, volume, instrumentation, mood, and so on, while still being identifiable as one pattern. If persons are patterns, they are of this sort.

However, the most significant point of our definition is that a person is "actions," not "stuff." Right here is quite a divergence from the customary methods of getting at God; most theology would define God in terms of his "being," essence, substance, inner nature, "stuff." What is he made out of?— to put it crudely. But even if we would take for granted that some sort of God-stuff lies behind what we identify as God-actions, how would you propose that we go about getting at it? And is it not just a little presumptuous for man even to pretend that he can "figure out" what God's inner nature must be? If there is any area in which human investigation is helpless, this is it. Why, you don't even know what person-stuff is in a human being, although presumably that is what you yourself are made of.

Consider; bones, meat, blood, and all such cannot be the true person-stuff. Dogs have all that but are not persons. What have you more than they? Carving it as closely as they have, scientists have not been able to locate anything remotely resembling a person-essence, whether it be called "soul" or something else. But we can do better and ask the man who owns one, namely, you. Have you, in your own experience as a person, ever felt, sensed, encountered, detected, or used anything you could describe as person-stuff? Along this line, the more I think, the less confident I am that I am.

How then do we distinguish between a dog and a person, or for that matter between one person and another (not simply between one "body" and another)? Definitely not through any perception or identification of essential "being" but through the perception and identification of *actions*. A person acts differently than a dog does. And "actions" we here intend in a very broad sense to include internalized acts—namely, thoughts—as well as the externalized acts of speech, deeds, and comportment. The person himself, of course, has some cognizance of both his inner and outward acts and would say that the latter proceed from the former. But regarding anyone except myself, I can only deduce the former from the latter. Yet either way (or both ways) the pattern of a person's *activity* is different from a dog's.

And this difference of action is what we refer to when we say that he *is* different; we cannot prove that this difference of action springs from some sort of a difference in "being." A person *is* what he does—and what he thinks is part of what he does. Mr. Smith undergoes a traumatic experience for good or for ill; subsequently his associates observe, "He's a *different* man!" Or, something is done, and a friend testifies: "Jones couldn't have done that; it isn't his character!" But these in no sense are judgments regarding changes of "being" but precisely comments on how the person *acts*.

Of the "being" of human persons we know nothing; and of the "being" of the God person we know even less. But of the actions both of human persons and of the God person we can begin to speak; so let us speak here where there is something to be said. Whether or not there is such a thing as God-stuff we can leave up to God.

The thinking in which we are here engaged is "ontological"; but whether we are *doing* ontology or *fighting* it is a matter of debate. "Ontology" derives from the Greek word for "being" and thus denotes thought concerning the essential being of things. Traditionally, then, ontology has trafficked in such

48

items as we listed earlier: being, essence, substance, hypostasis, inner nature, stuff. But of late ontology has been broken open to include almost anything and everything; "being" no longer has any very precise connotation but seems to refer to whatever is most fundamental and significant about the entity in question.

So according to today's rules, ontology is the name of our game, for we certainly are trying to get to the nitty-gritty of what persons are—both human persons and the God person. Yet, I am confident, most people still think of "being" in terms of the earlier, more precise understanding; and our contention is that "person" never can be adequately defined through such ontological categories. Ours, then, is a non-ontological ontology that speaks of function and action rather than of being as such. In scientific terms, ours is an "operational" ontology (if ontology it must be called). The interest of scientists has tended more and more to shift away from the attempt to discover *what* things are and to be content with discovering *how* they operate. And we submit that such an approach to "person" will both open new possibilities of understanding and at the same time get us to the most foundamental truth about persons.

A person is an identifiable pattern of actions. But there are many configurations that can be identified as patterns of action which are not persons. True; and so we must specify what

49

sort of pattern it is that qualifies as a person-pattern. It is as if plotting the actions of a dog always produced a wavy graph and those of a person a jagged graph. What are the characteristic marks of *person*-pattern?

In the first place, person-actions speak of conscious decision, choice, freedom, will, self-determination. In the second place and closely related, the actions of a person form a pattern which denotes purpose, forethought, planning, intelligence, significance in terms of a long-range goal (perhaps what we earlier called "eschatological perspective"?). In the third place and perhaps most basic, a person-pattern manifests what the first impulse might be to call "self-awareness" but which can be described more accurately. The second impulse is to call it "the awareness of others," but even this is not precise enough. It is the awareness of the possibility of establishing and enjoying relationships between oneself and other persons. A person-pattern thus shows the desire to open oneself, to communicate, to reach out; and consequently the activities which most clearly denote *person*-action are speech (word), love, hate, command, promise, blessing, curse, forgiveness, faith, mistrust —relational actions all.

There is a fourth mode that must be included as person-action, although it is not easy to define and may be simply the intensification of our third. Persons demonstrate "presence," the ability to "be with" another person in a loving and creative way. Such presence may or may not involve bodily at-handedness; it may or may not be manifested through overt actions; but through it a person "presents himself" to another, deliberately makes himself available and accessible. And this, by the way, is one of the strongest qualities of God's person-hood.

Whenever, then, we encounter a pattern of actions that are free, purposed, communicative, and "presentative," there is "a person." Note carefully: the person *is* the actions themselves and not the fellow behind them, the performer of them. Don't fall back into the idea that behind the actions there must be an essence which is more basic than the actions themselves; remember that we don't know anything about a person-essence.

We have said that the person *is* his actions. However, the fact that those actions form *a pattern* makes it necessary and right to modify that statement—and in a way that might seem to undercut all we have been saying and put us right back into an ontology of "being." So our thought must be very precise at this point. A person, we now must say, is *one who acts* according to the modes that we have defined as person-actions. But to allow in that little "one who" immediately calls up visions of a lump of "being" which is the source of the actions, immediately invites us to ask, "Who is this 'one'? What does he look like? What is he made of?"

But we do not intend all that much with our word "one" and firmly resist all curious desire to open that Pandora's box. We mean "one" in a quite literal sense and without all the implications that usually accompany it when it is applied to a person. That there is a "one" who acts is a way of affirming the *integrity* of these actions; they are the actions of a "one" rather than of a "many" or of a "none" (a "random"). The actions of a true person are patterned so as to display integrity, coherency, consistency, totality. A person, then, is an actor, or agent; but as much as can be said about his "being," about *what* an actor is, is that an actor is *one* who acts. So even to call a person "one who" is still to be speaking operationally of his actions rather than ontologically of his being. And with that our emphasis is right back where it started: all one can know about persons—and all one need know—concerns how they *act*.

In due course we will get to the fellow behind, to something like "essence," but we will discover that he (or it) is far from "essential," being indeed somewhat extraneous to the whole idea of "a person."

What is a person like? A person is like a melody—every person is, not just the pretty girls among us. Each person is his own, is the particular pattern that is his tune—"Here We Go Round the Mulberry Bush," for example. It is the distinctive arrangement of his tune-pattern that makes an individual

52

an individual, although his tune must display the general character described above if he is to qualify as a person. "Person," then, is the generic term including all the individual action-tunes of one type, say, nursery songs. And under these terms God is a person, is fully and literally a person—as fully and literally as you are. He is an identifiable action-pattern displaying all the person qualifications; he has—rather, he *is*—his own distinctive melody, say, "Three Blind Mice" (no trinitarian implications intended).

Notice that we consistently have called God "*a* person" and would be willing to call him "an individual." There are philosophers who are ready to identify him as "Person" but quite unwilling to call him "*a* person." Now what "Person" is, I haven't the slightest idea. According to our analogy it would be similar to "Melody." But is there such a thing as "Melody"? I suppose there must be—as an abstraction in the minds of philosophers. But "Melody" as such must be about the most unreal and useless thing imaginable—if indeed it is even imaginable. It is certain that no one ever has played nor anyone ever heard "Melody"; all that can be played or heard is a melody, or melodies. If "Melody" were to mean anything more than an idea, a mental construct in someone's head, I suppose it would have to consist in banging all the keys of the piano at once and letting each listener pick out the particular melody he wanted to hear. And this is about where

53

some concepts of God come out: whang the keyboard of the universe, listen to the pandemonium, and somewhere there is the communication, the reaching out of God. No, the only God who can provide anything like eschatological perspective must be somewhat more focused and concrete, must be *a* person, an individual.

In fact, if anyone deserves to be called a person, *"one who,"* it is God. I am trying to be a person—and not doing too well at it. I keep hitting accidental notes that louse up my "Here We Go Round" melody; my timing and pitch get all off; and I can't play the tune twice the same way. I sound to myself and, I am sure, to other people like competing persons rather than a person; my name, as yours, is Legion. But have you heard "Three Blind Mice"? There is what can be called a melody! "One who knows what he himself is," as Kierkegaard put it.

But what, very precisely, is a melody? There is still more to be milked from this analogy. A melody is a pattern of sound vibrations. Not quite; there is more that must be said. Consider that Beethoven, when stone deaf, completely impervious to sound vibrations, was still a pretty good man with a melody. A melody is a pattern *normally* carried on sound vibrations but capable of being carried on other media as well. Was "Row, Row, Row Your Boat" any less "Row, Row, Row Your Boat" when it existed only in the mind of its composer, before ever it had been committed to sound vibrations? Is its identity any different when it rides the carrier of human thought, or notes on a staff, or radio waves, or a wiggly line on an oscilloscope? Clearly, the essence of a melody resides in its patternhood and not in the "stuff" that carries it. Carrier it must have, and one carrier there is that is its "natural"; but a melody definitely is not determined by its carrier and is not necessarily confined to one sort of carrier.

We must be careful here, for we are turning usual ways of thinking on their head. With persons, as with melodies, their "essence" (the stuff of which they are made) is not "essential" to their being (if "being" is the proper term here). The very absurdity of that statement, if read according to the traditional canons of philosophical theology, is an indication of the revolution we are trying to pull off. Let's make it even more maddening: with a person, his "accidents" (his actions and manifestations) are his "essence," and his "essence" (his inner "being") is accidental.

The natural carrier for personhood is, of course, the human body. Here is where we customarily encounter the action-pattern which we know as "a person"; it is the actions of a human body that are configured into a person-pattern as it is air vibrations that are patterned into a melody. Yet even here within the natural realm we find personhood (at least to a limited extent) patterned in other media as well. For instance, there is a husband who has been away from home for some time, say, in the service. One day he receives a package in the mail, opens it to find a lovely cake, and exclaims, "That's my wife!"—and nobody laughs. As regards the common use of those words, the statement should be sheer nonsense. But it is not; the man is saying that in the whole event-entity of receiving the cake he discerns the action-pattern which he knows as the person of his wife.

Granted, the action-pattern of the cake can be traced back directly to its source in the particular human body that always has been associated with her person. As far as the person of a man is concerned, we do not discover his pattern being "played" independently of his body, although that body can become the agent for impressing the person-pattern onto other media. Thus, even if a human body (which term we mean as including the flesh, psyche, mind, spirit—the whole works) is the *necessary* carrier of a man's person-pattern, this does not imply that the pattern and the carrier are the same thing by any means. Indeed, cases such as that of the cake-wife at least hint that person-pattern is conceivable as being carried via media other than and independent of the human body.

"A man," then, could be defined as an individualized person-pattern necessarily configured by a human body. "God," conversely, would be an individualized person-pattern the configuration of which is not limited to a human body; he is, neither more nor less, a *super*natural person.

But when we call God "an individualized person-pattern" we intend those words in precisely the same sense as when we apply them to a man. Of course, God's melody is his own (and we would be quick to say, the most beautiful rendition ever heard) and in this sense unique. But every person's melody is unique in this sense. Consider that by the very nature of things any and every melody *has* to be unique; the same melody heard a second time is not a *second* melody identical with the first; it is the *one* melody which merely has been replayed. God is a person, then, in exactly the same sense that men are; his categorical uniqueness comes with the freedom of that person-pattern to find its configuration in media other than the human body.

We need to be very careful at this point. We dare not fall into the simplistic trap of thinking of personhood as an independent, free-floating "something" which then becomes attached to or incorporated in the "something else" which is its carrier. Neither the God person nor men persons are fleas looking for a dog to call home. Although every bit as specific and concrete (as "existential") as any "thing" that ever was, a pattern is not a "thing" in any sense of the term; and it is extremely awkward to speak about the "being" of a pattern.

A pattern is its carrier *put into arrangement.* Now certainly

the carrier arranged is something different from the carrier unarranged—something vastly different. But this is not because
a new, separate "something" has been added. Don't even
try to think of pattern apart from a carrier; it will drive you
crazy. In a very true sense there is no such thing as "a pattern,"
there is only some "thing" patterned. And so, with God as
with every other person, there has to be a carrier before his
personhood even is conceivable—although the carrier is not
the personhood. Thus God is free but not free-floating; that
is, he is not confined to one carrier, but carrier he must have.

And what is the carrier (better, the carriers) of God? Well,
some ancient Hebrews listened carefully to their history (something it wouldn't hurt more of us to do) and, lo and behold,
they heard not the unarranged smash and clatter that most
men hear; within their history they heard a melody, a person-
melody. Nor was it vague, almost formless music—maybe.
It was a tune one could whistle: "Three Blind Mice." Some
of the dominant notes were grace, promise, law, redemption,
covenant, lordship. We will not attempt a detailed transcrip-
tion of the song—the Bible does that very well—but it should
be considered that the notes we have named are free, purposed, relational, presentative actions all—precisely what we
earlier defined as constituting *person*-pattern. These men could
not escape the conclusion that they were in the presence of

58

"a person," for the melody heard in their history was that of a Person par excellence.

Then, turning to the world of nature, these Hebrews heard at least echoes of the same tune. It sounded much fainter and less precise—so much so that only their previous familiarity with the song enabled them to say that here also was to be heard "Three Blind Mice." But they did testify that God's person-melody was in nature as well as in history.

The conviction that our history is continuous with that Hebrew history; that, by listening to it, history still evinces "Three Blind Mice" for us today; that the melody is so integral to history that it will play as long as there is a history in which to play—this is the conviction we express when we speak of God the Father. The God-melody as heard in nature also is included under this head. God the Father, then, is God's person-pattern as perceived in the carrier of history and nature. And it is the pattern carried thus that is particularly relevant to our earlier discussion of eschatological perspective. Here is the supernatural person who transcends "the middle" to cover history in its totality—eschatological beginning and end as well as present middle.

Then there lived a man; and one day his followers turned to one another and said, "Listen! Listen to that man! Not only is his a real great person-melody, that is 'Three Blind Mice' if ever we heard it. Listen to it loud, clear, and sweet—easier even for human ears to follow than by listening to history." With these followers, this is the conviction we express when we speak of God the Son. God the Son is God's person-pattern as perceived through the "natural" carrier of the human body of Jesus of Nazareth.

Is the Son truly God? Indeed so; in every sense of the word. His person is a second playing of the very same melody that men had known as God the Father; and this is what it means to *be* God. Is the Son truly man? Certainly. Entirely and without remainder he fits our definition of man: an individualized person-pattern, the configuration of which is limited to a human body.

What we have accomplished, then, is to set our terms in such a way that there is no reason why God cannot be a man. We have opened the way for a Christology which eliminates the old, awkward ploys of importing from some other "where" some other sort of "stuff" known as the "being" of God, of talking about two "natures" in one person (whatever "natures" are), of concocting such an incomprehensible "explanation" as *anhypostasis*. As soon as we start thinking of personhood as pattern rather than substance, all sorts of old problems begin solving themselves.

Finally, because these followers of Jesus got so good at hearing "Three Blind Mice" in him, they discovered that after his song was over the melody lingered on. They continued to hear the tune in their own personal experience and particularly in their fellowship with one another. Here was a third, real, and distinctive "playing" of God that proceeded from that of the Father and of the Son. And we affirm this conviction of Jesus' followers when we speak of God the Holy Spirit. God the Holy Spirit is God's person-pattern perceived in the personal experience of individuals and groups.

One God in three persons? No; our terminology will not allow us to say that. What we can and do say is: God's one person-pattern found in three different carrier-media. The unity of God lies precisely in his "person" and not in a "substance" of which we know nothing and can know nothing.

What we have come to, then, is a God who is truly supernatural—yet without many of the customary impedimenta of that term. God can act supernaturally toward us and communicate a supernatural perspective to us without our experiencing or it being necessary for us to posit either supernatural substance or a supernatural location. Because the carriers of the God-pattern are: (a) history and nature, (b) the body of the man Jesus, and (c) our personal experiences as individuals and in groups; everything we know of God comes via *natural* means, as this-worldly phenomena. And yet the communication, the pattern, therein perceived speaks *super*naturally, speaks of more than the present actuality of this world.

Our first impulse is to want to account for this "more" by

61

thinking of the pattern as the "work" of a Being made of other than natural stuff and living in an other than natural place. But resist the impulse; it does not follow. The person *is* the pattern, not the ghostly worker of the pattern. Precisely in his pattern *is* God and his "super" nature; there is no need to go further to an invisible Superbody formed out of invisible Superstuff living in an invisible Superworld.

This may seem like an extraordinarily difficult way to think (or to *stop* thinking), but we do it every day as regards human persons, so it ought not be impossible as regards the God person. Anyone will testify concerning a person he knows (and particularly one whom he *loves)* that that person is very much more than all that the natural sciences can discover within him or tell us about him. And yet in order to explain that "more" we do not take recourse to a theory about his constitution including nonphysical "stuff" to which the sciences have no access. (Earlier men used to, with their concept of the substantial soul, but this has been proved unbiblical in the first place and unnecessary in the second.) No, the "more" which science cannot explain is precisely the person's pattern of action, and this pattern of action is precisely what we come to know and appreciate in the process of loving him. His actions, of course, are never independent of his physical constitution, but also they never can be explained simply by analyzing that physical constitution.

62

Man, thus, is a person-pattern who *is* more than his carrier (his psycho-physical body) yet without "having" any*thing* more than that body. And God is a person-pattern who *is* more than his carrier (the world of natural phenomena) yet without "having" any*thing* supernatural.

AN EXCURSUS ON HERESY

An excursus is a device by which an author can say something that is not quite germane but which he wants to say anyhow. Many authors write them without being honest enough to admit what they are doing.

Is our doctrine of person and of God as "a person" heretical or is it orthodox?—not that the question of heresy is of any great moment in the new theology, but it is something to consider in any case.

It all depends upon what one understands by "orthodox." My own considered opinion is that we have portrayed a God who is capable of displaying all the qualities and performing all the acts that the biblical faith ascribes to him—which is more than can be said for many doctrines of God. Neither have we ascribed to him either a character or characteristics foreign to biblical thought. If the Bible is the criterion, this understanding in our judgment is orthodox.

It must be admitted, however, that our explanation plays

hob with the historic creeds. They all attempt to explain deity in terms of substance (being, essence); we have rejected that approach entirely and made substance, at best, an aspect of God's carrier-media and not his personhood.

What we are trying to pull off—if we can say so modestly —is an Einsteinian revolution in theology. The pre-Einstein situation in physics was this:

"The nineteenth century physicists, who were very mechanistic in their outlook, felt quite sure that the propagation of waves predicted by Maxwell's equations [i.e. light waves, radio waves, x-rays, etc.] requires the existence of a propagation medium. Just as water waves propagate through water, so, according to their argument, electromagnetic waves must propagate through a medium. This medium was given the name *ether*. The ether was obliged to have somewhat strange properties in order not to disagree with certain known facts. For instance, the ether must be massless since it was observed that electromagnetic waves such as light can travel through a vacuum. [It must also, of course, be invisible, unsmellable, unfeelable, etc., and yet omnipresent, permeating the whole universe.] However, it must have elastic properties in order to be able to sustain the vibrations which are inherent in the idea of wave motion. Despite these difficulties, the concept of the ether was considerably more attractive than the alternative, which was to assume that electromagnetic disturbances could be propagated without the aid of a propagation medium." [2]

Since the days when the Nicene fathers started formulating creeds, as an inheritance from Greek philosophy, formal theology has had its own ether theory, the ontological concept of "being." When an ontologist, Paul Tillich for example, speaks in such terms as, "Certainly we belong to being—its power is in us—otherwise we would not be. But we are also separated from it; we do not possess it fully. Our power of being is limited. We are a mixture of being and nonbeing," [3] it sounds, if we may say so, very "ethereal."

And theology's ether theory turns out to be vastly more complicated than that of physics, because it has had to posit several different kinds of ether (being). In addition to "being-ether," there has to be—as Tillich's statement implies—the "nonbeing-ether" that makes up the other half of what I am. There has to be a unique "God-ether" so that the Son can be "of one substance" with the Father. (And if you who are human cannot begin to describe even the human-ether of which you are constituted, then God-ether must be something etherealized beyond all conception. No wonder people are becoming suspicious of it.) Then there also has to be a "divine-

[2] Robert Martin Eisberg, *Fundamentals of Modern Physics* (New York: John Wiley, 1961), pp. 7-8.
[3] Paul Tillich, *Biblical Religion and the Search for Ultimate Reality* (Chicago: University of Chicago Press, 1955), p. 11.

nature-ether" and a "human-nature-ether" so that Christ can combine the two natures in one person (and his human-nature-ether must be *impersonal* so that the "personhood" of his one person can be made entirely out of divine-nature-ether). And presumably dogs are of a different ether than humans are—and so on down the line.

Our intention is not to make traditional ontological theory look silly. It is not silly (better, it *was* not silly in its own day). Just as physics, when done within a mechanistic frame of reference, *had* to have an ether theory in order to make its electromagnetic computations come out right, so theology, with its ontological frame of reference, *had* to posit different kinds of "being" in order fully to express the Christian gospel. What Einstein did was to show that by thinking within a different frame of reference one eliminates all need for ether. And perhaps, theologically, our concept of person as melody will help solve the problem which Hughes Mearns did not state quite this way:

> As with the scholars I did stare,
> I saw some "stuff" that wasn't there.
> It wasn't there again today.
> Oh, how I wish 'twould go away!

However, under the terms of creedal theology, our doctrine would have to be categorized as "modalism"—which the church condemned as heresy. Even so, that condemnation was based on the assumption that the "being" behind a given pattern (mode) of action was more fundamental and primary than the action itself. The concern was that the deity of the various persons of the Trinity be rooted in that which was primary and not simply in the secondary. But conversely, we have argued that, at least as far as persons are concerned, the action-pattern is more basic than any "being" involved. And thus we too have been interested in basing deity in that which is most primary. Although our language is the direct contrary of that of the creeds, perhaps our intent is not wholly different. In any event, we are not about to *volunteer* for the burning—and would hope to be convicted on biblical rather than creedal grounds.

AN EXCURSUS ON HEARING "THREE BLIND MICE"

Our conception of God, when assisted by Kierkegaard, can throw considerable light on the problem of faith and the relation of faith to historical event and evidence. "Faith" is the hearing of "Three Blind Mice"; how does one go about it?

We have defined as an essential characteristic of person-pattern "the intent to communicate, to present oneself to another." If no such intent actually is present, then no person is present. "Three Blind Mice" cannot be heard unless it is being played; anyone who thinks he hears it when it is not being played is befooling himself. In short, faith does not *create* a God for itself but is true only as response to an actual communication from another. No matter how much "subjectivity" we may introduce into faith hereafter, it always must base back upon this completely "objective" address. And insofar as history of one sort or another is the carrier of God, God is actual only if the events and actions perceived as his person-pattern are actual historical events. Likewise, insofar as the human body of Jesus was a carrier of God, there has to have been the man Jesus, and he has to have acted as the gospel proclaims him as having acted, if the God of his person-pattern was actual. So too with the Holy Spirit.

But, it must be noted, even where there is complete agreement as to the factuality and character of the historical carrier involved, there is no implication of similar agreement as to the presence of pattern. If the melody is not being played, it cannot be heard; but even assuming that it is being played, it is not equally "hearable" to all listeners. Oh, I suppose that if the God-melody was in fact as simple and obvious as "Three Blind Mice," then a careful, objective analysis of the sound waves could be said to "prove" that an intentional communication-pattern was present. But because the God-melody is infinitely more subtle and complex—like something by Bela

68

Bartok—the distinction between "noise" and "melody" becomes a fine one, and one which ultimately no amount of analysis can decide.

The listeners may be in agreement as to what the sound wave looks like, what amplitudes, frequencies, and intervals are involved. They all may have equally good hearing; the issue is not one of sensory or historical perceptivity. But whether or not that sound represents an intentional communication-pattern is something which in the final analysis cannot be determined on an objective basis. This is what Kierkegaard meant by saying that truth, faith-truth, is subjectivity; he was not for a moment denying that the communication-pattern must have objective reality.

What then makes the difference between the person who, upon listening to Bartok, hears melody and the person who, listening to the same sounds, hears noise? The matter of education is involved, but education itself in this instance comes down finally to whether the listener *wants* to hear music or not. It is not that the desire to hear melody *creates* melody; this we have not said. But given the objective presence of melody, it depends upon the subjective decision of the listener as to whether he will hear it *as melody* or not.

This decision is what Kierkegaard calls "the leap of faith." But notice that it is nothing akin to a blind jump in the dark, as many would have it. It is a clear-headed, well-defined decision dealing directly with good historical evidence. Indeed, the decision *not* to hear the sound as melody is the leap of unfaith just as much as the opposite decision is the leap of faith.

All this has something to say apropos the death-of-God theology. Such a theologian can say that *he* does not hear "Three Blind Mice" either in history, Jesus, or his own personal experience. He can go beyond this to say that his researches indicate that very many modern men do not hear this melody. But he has a right to transpose those observations into the objective claim, "God is dead," only if he can convince us that he and these others have *wanted* to hear the melody, sincerely have tried to hear the melody and been unable to. But this is precisely the impression these theologians do not give; anyone who truly had wanted to hear the God-melody and been disappointed would show a little more *Angst* than they are able to muster. Those theologians who start with the presupposition that man does not need God are no more competent to judge whether God is dead or alive than the man who hates music is competent to judge whether Bartok represents noise or melody.

Also, within the context of our understanding of God, the matter of "miracle" takes on a different aspect. As with "faith," it is Kierkegaard who has given us the cue.

70

In the first place, a miracle cannot now be what it often has been thought of as being, an intrusion into the this-worldly nexus of some other "stuff" or some other "body" from some other "where." Our whole argument has been designed to eliminate the need for positing such spatio-temporal "otherness."

But Kierkegaard pointed out that *in the first place* a miracle is not even "a miracle," that is, it is not a demonstration by God or a manifestation of God that is unimpeachably and self-evidently such. No, in the first place a miracle is simply a freak happening, a strange coincidence, an inexplicable occurrence. Perhaps even the the term "inexplicable" is not quite accurate here; "very difficult to explicate" would be better, for events of this sort do take place every day of the world, and for many (if not all) of these we do come up with "explanations" of some sort—even if many of the explanations must be about as far-fetched as the occurrences themselves and give a very great deal of credit to the role of chance.

Yet not even those incidents for which we can find *no* explanation do we automatically take as being miracles of God. Instead, the decisive qualification is: Do you hear this event as a playing of "Three Blind Mice"? Does it sound like a communication of the God person? And, of course, there are some events of very obvious "explanation" which nevertheless are heard as renditions of the God-melody. But even so, whether any particular event—no matter how spectacular and inexplicable—is to be heard as noise or as melody cannot be decided on the basis of the self-evident character of the event itself.

Thus, for example, Hugh Schonfield's *The Passover Plot* is a *possible* explanation of the historical evidence which customarily has been explained as the resurrection of Jesus. Schonfield's explanation is fantastic, to be sure, although no more so *(and no less so)* than the explanation that God raised Jesus from the dead. The point is that the facts of the case are such as to force one to a "fantastic" explanation of one kind or another, into a "leap," whether of faith or unfaith. Which way the leap will go depends not upon the self-evident character of the historical evidence (which is "inexplicable" by normal canons) but upon whether or not one hears "Three Blind Mice" within the event. And whether or not one hears this melody depends, as we suggested earlier, upon whether one *chooses* to hear it as melody or not.

A miracle, then, is not *in the first place* "a miracle"; it is, rather, simply an inexplicable occurrence, the very inexplicability of which compels one to give it attention, to listen; it could be communication from God (or it could be nothing more than one of the many freakish things that happen in our world). A miracle, then, becomes such only upon the hearing of faith. To call the event "a miracle" is not to come to an

72

explanation *demanded* by the facts, any more than Schonfield's explanation is *demanded* by the facts; it is, through faith, to affirm one of the possible explanations *afforded* by the facts. A miracle cannot *compel* faith; it does compel attention to a situation in which a decision either for faith or against faith must be made.[4]

[4] For a fuller and more technical discussion of this view of faith and miracle, see my article, "Fact, Faith, and Foolishness: Kierkegaard and the New Quest," *The Journal of Religion,* January, 1968.

CHAPTER FIVE

DRAMATIS PERSONAE: GOD, MAN, AND MEMBERS OF THE COMPANY

There is a very telling objection that could be raised at this point; namely, that we have overshot ourselves. In order to satisfy man's need for eschatological perspective, an orientation point, it hardly was necessary to go so far as positing God as *a person*, as one whose actions are marked by freedom and decision, by planning and goal-seeking, by the attempt to communicate with and respond to other persons, by the desire to be "present with" man. We have provided much more God than the problem required.

The objection is entirely valid, but it is such only because we did not do a complete job of describing man's need in those earlier chapters. Now, with the help of our concept of "person" we are ready to return to the previous order of business.

Obviously it does not take "a person" to be a beacon in the jungle; a less than personal God could satisfy that discussion. We did also speak of God the Playwright, but that was something of a red herring. Although saying "playwright," we actually were speaking of man's need for a script. The two are not the same, nor does the one necessarily imply the other; we all have heard about the how-many thousand monkeys that wrote the plays of Shakespeare. But what exactly is the nature of the orientation that man needs? Is it the sort that a beacon or script could provide, or does it call for something more?

The consideration which inevitably lies behind all thinking about God is: What is the most problematic aspect of human existence? What is the most basic question for which men seek an answer?

Many theologians would say that it is the ontological question, the question of being. Paul Tillich put the matter thus:

"Philosophy is that cognitive endeavor in which the question of being is asked. . . . The question of being is not the question of any special being, its existence and nature, but it is the question of what it means to *be*. It is the simplest, most profound, and absolutely inexhaustible question—the question of what it means to say that something *is*. This word 'is' hides the riddle of all riddles, the mystery that there is anything at all. Every philosophy, whether it asks the question of being openly or not, moves around this mystery. . . . Philosophy in this sense is not a matter of liking or disliking. It is a matter of man as man, for man is that being who asks the question of being." [1]

But if man is that being who asks the question of being, then apparently Tillich didn't think there were very many men among us, for later in the same book he complains that the average man doesn't even know enough to ask the question of being:

"There is an element in the biblical and ecclesiastical idea of God which makes the ontological question necessary. It is the assertion that God *is*. Of course not everyone asks what this word 'is' in relation to God means. Most people, including the biblical writers, take the word in its popular sense: something 'is' if it can be found in the whole of potential experience. That which can be encountered within the whole of reality is real." [2]

We submit that Tillich's second statement is correct; it is not "men" but "philosophers" who ask the question of being

[1] *Biblical Religion and the Search for Ultimate Reality*, pp. 5-6, 8.
[2] *Ibid.*, p. 82.

76

—and even they must go through years of training before they are able so much as to think the question, let alone strive to answer it. For if Tillich is to be taken for what he says in the first passage, then he believes that man's most basic need and desire is to solve "the mystery of being." Yet in the second quotation he as much as says that most people—including the biblical authors—achieve their Christian faith on the basis of a rather definite understanding of "is" (even though it be one that Tillich deems inadequate) and without expressing any particular concern to go beyond it. If we may say so, it is a bit difficult to understand the Christian faith as being primarily the answer to a need of which neither the formulators of that faith nor ninety percent of its followers show any cognizance. There must be a more "existential" need to which the faith is addressed—or else "being" is used here in a sense so broad and vague that it can include whatever else might be said.

So we deny that "being" is the basic question man asks of God or anyone else and gladly take our stand with the "biblical writers" and the "most people" whom Tillich decries. In any case, our concept of God as a person uses "is" entirely in its popular sense; God "is" and "is" only because his melody can be heard "in the whole of potential experience."

We are getting much closer to the fact of the matter when we turn to someone like the psychologist Viktor Frankl, who asserts that man's is basically a search for *meaning*. Man can endure anything and is willing to go to all lengths if only he can become convinced that there is some overarching significance in what he is doing and what is happening to him. All we said earlier about orientation and eschatological perspective relates beautifully at this point.

But although what Frankl says is true, he has not yet said enough. "Meaning" would suggest that what man needs most is a script, information, intellectual enlightenment. ("Meaning," of course, can be taken to imply *more than* simply intellectual content, yet certainly it must include at least some content. The word, however, does not necessarily imply the element of person-to-Person relationship upon which we shall insist.)

Ultimately, as regards the course of the world itself, the search for "meaning" could suggest that man's greatest need is for information regarding the end-state of history. But the Christian gospel has never pretended to provide this, and those who would use the Bible as a sourcebook of apocalyptic speculation regarding the when, how, and where of the end-time are both misusing scripture and contradicting Jesus.

Now, to be sure, the gospel does carry with it some basic insights about the end-state—although not in the way of a detailed script. It is crucial, however, that the end-state is called "the kingdom of God"; it can be understood in no other

78

terms than as a situation in which God's will being done is completely and in very truth the fact of the matter. This means that the end-state will be characterized by the qualities that always have marked God's ruling, namely, his grace, his mercy, his justice, and his love. When it is further specified that Jesus Christ is the agent of this kingdom, its character is made just that much more explicit; the "style" of the end-state will be the style of Jesus of Nazareth.

But even this information, in and of itself, is not the key to the kingdom nor to eschatological perspective. To make it so would be to slip into gnosticism (salvation through having the inside dope). However, there is a possibility that goes quite beyond this and all other _information_ regarding the end. If that end is to be the _de facto_ situation of God's ruling, then the one effective way of getting eschatological perspective is by letting God start to rule here and now; orientation toward the Person of the End is a much more live and promising alternative than trying to get a picture of the end.

Thus man's search for "meaning" cannot be the whole story; man can get along without "answers" as long as he feels assured that Someone who has the answers is working at the job. This is the basic insight of the book of Job. Job got no eschatological script that told him how his trials were going to turn out, no explanation of the "why" of his suffering. And any explanation necessarily would have to have been limited to his own power of comprehension. No, Job got something much greater, a face-to-face meeting with the One who not only possessed the information but who *was* the meaning and who was personally concerned about Job.

Consider that a small child can be quite willing to face even a very traumatic experience (such as an operation) which is entirely beyond his comprehension simply in the knowledge that Daddy and Mommy say that this is the right thing to happen. To know the One Who Really Truly Cares is a deeper need than is a detailed explanation of what life and history are all about (which there is no guarantee that man could comprehend in any case). In this regard, a modern ballad in the folk idiom perhaps speaks truer than any theological disquisition could:

> Don't know where I'm goin',
>   And I don't know where I've been,
> Don't know where I'll be—
>   But until then
> I'll just ramble round the country,
>   Travelin' here and there,
> Tryin' to find someone,
>   One Who Really Truly Cares.
>
> In this world of trouble,
>   Trouble all around,

Love's the only answer——
   It's what I haven't found.
Someday, somewhere,
   I'll find someone who cares,
One who really loves me,
   One Who Really Truly Cares.

Why are some men freer?
   And why do some men die?
Why do children suffer?
   And why do children cry?
Oh, I don't want to see this;
   First I'd rather die.
So I'll just ramble on,
   Travelin' here and there,
Tryin' to find someone,
   One Who Really Truly Cares.[3]

We have made free to capitalize a few letters herein, because, if the one who really truly cares is only another man in the middle, he cannot provide the eschatological perspective that our condition wants, cannot speak to the eschatological concerns of the concluding stanza. Man does need to find among human persons some ones who really truly care, but

[3] Linda Kerr, "One Who Cares." Copyright © 1967 by Linda Kerr.

these do not obviate the need for his also finding the super-natural Person who can represent the meaning of the whole. Men in the middle caring for one another (even if it were possible for them to achieve this through their own initiative) still fall short of constituting the kingdom of God.

All we have just said comes under our earlier rubric of "orientation"; it is simply that the sort of orientation man requires can be provided only by a Person and not by a beacon or script. Jesus' parable of the prodigal son can help us here. What was it that the prodigal needed and the loving father gave him? The son thought it was the means of livelihood—food, drink, clothing, and shelter. But he was wrong; his father was not the only one who could have provided that; the son was not starving to death, nor had he exhausted every means of staying alive; he wanted to use his father as a *deus ex machina*. But the father (getting the jump on Bonhoeffer's dictum that man doesn't need *this* God) was wise enough to distinguish between the false need which the son voiced and the real need that the boy had not sufficient self-knowledge to voice. What did the father give the son? Not simply the ring and fatted calf—these are symbols. He gave the sonship, the relationship to himself which the boy earlier had rejected; this is what the prodigal really needed if the rest of his world was to come right.

"Sonship." Notice first of all that this is a relational term which makes sense only within a person-and-person context. In the second place it is an orientational term that tells me who I am, where I stand in the nexus of my relationships. However, it might be objected, it speaks of an orientation *to* God; whereas it is in man's orientation *to the world* that we have been finding his greatest need.

But consider: an orientation point is precisely that which is so situated that when I am rightly oriented toward it, I also am rightly oriented toward the world which it organizes; it has no other function. Turn to the world? Certainly; but the only way to accomplish that maneuver is to turn to the God who is our orientation toward the world. If we may put it thus, all in the world the new theology needs to learn is to teeter as it totters.

The new theology talks a great deal about man's lordship over the world. This is a valid emphasis of the gospel, but it needs to be teetered a bit if it is to be truly of the good news. A more accurate and more dialectical way of putting the matter is that man has been placed in *sonship* to the One who is *Lord* of the world. This amounts to man's having a lordship over the world but makes it clear that that lordship can succeed only as long as it remains in sonship to God. It is in his relation to God that man gets pointed right for his relationships to the world.

There is another need of God about which the prodigal

son story speaks, about which the church has talked much, but about which we as yet have said nothing. What about forgiveness? We submit that we have been right in speaking first and foremost of eschatological perspective and introducing forgiveness only at this point, because forgiveness is a rather funny thing. It is a need of the second order, as it were, that cannot even exist except in relation to a prior need.

Consider that the prodigal could have obviated all his feeling of need for forgiveness by the simple expedient of staying away from his father. It was only when his need for his father became so acute that he *had* to go home that the fact of his alienation and the corresponding need for forgiveness became pressing. And even then, this need for forgiveness, far from being of the sort that would draw him to his father, tended to keep him away. Only his prior and fundamental need for his father created the need for forgiveness and made him willing to face up to it. He could not need forgiveness half so much needed he not sonship more.

Here then is the context that makes sense of Bonhoeffer's protest against approaching men for Christ by trying to convince them that they are sinners who need forgiveness. Would Bonhoeffer deny or gloss over the fact of universal sin and subsequently the universal need for forgiveness? Not for a moment; but this way is singularly ineffective in helping men to God. The surest way of *keeping* the prodigal in the far

country is to tell him that he has to ask his father for forgiveness—when he doesn't feel the need to go home in any case.
No, help the boy see the advantages of the eschatological
perspective of sonship and feel the need for such; once he
gets headed home, the realization that reconciliation with his
father entails a need for forgiveness will arise of itself. Then
is the proper moment for the proclamation of forgiving grace;
earlier it does not make sense.

Man's need for God does not arise in the first place out of
the fact that he is a sinner but simply out of the fact that he
is a creature, a man in the middle. The recognition of this need
must come first; from it naturally will follow the recognition
that he also is a sinner in need of forgiveness—precisely because he has denied his own creatureliness and his need of
God's help. Bonhoeffer is right; and it is not that sin and
forgiveness are to be omitted, but that first things must come
first.

But back to our proper theme, the case can be made that
the total ministry of Jesus points directly to the need and function of God that we are here developing. Central to Jesus'
message, modern scholarship is agreed, was his proclamation
of the coming of the kingdom of God. Now the coming of the
kingdom is nothing more than the course of this world seen
from the eschatological perspective of the One who is its Lord
and King. The invitation to enter and live out of this kingdom

which presently is in process of realization speaks, then, precisely to man's deepest need—the need to rise above the middle by fixing upon the orientation point which can give organization to the totality of life and history, which can enable man to move into the future in hope and in victory.

The very concept "the kingdom of God" speaks of God as an orientation point, but there is a second, equally important emphasis in Jesus' message—this having to do with the *nature of man's relationship* to this God who is his orientation point. A number of contemporary scholars (among whom Joachim Jeremias is predominant) have noted the significance of the fact that Jesus addressed God as *Abba* and that the early church was enough impressed that it carried the Aramaic term over into Greek usage without translating it. *Abba* is the most intimate and elemental Aramaic word by which a child could address his father; "Papa" or "Daddy" would be the closest equivalent in English. And the evidence is that no Jew before Jesus ever had the nerve to talk to God in this way. Jesus did; and the fact that the Lord's Prayer seems originally to have opened *Abba* indicates that he taught his disciples to do so as well.

To call God *Abba* speaks of a new and unique relationship to him—one of a special affinity of love based upon a special affinity of will demonstrated in a special quality of obedience. And the New Testament understanding rather clearly is that, because Jesus had this unique relationship to God, those who are in Christ share it with him and have been granted the gracious privilege of themselves knowing God as *Abba*. But the important point for our present discussion is that this central aspect of Jesus' message points to the nature of God as "a person"—and as a Person Who Really Truly Cares—in about as strong a way as can be done. Likewise it emphasizes the close, very much person-to-Person quality of man's relationship to that God. It is difficult to see how any concept of God that makes him less than a person—or attempts to make him more than a person (as though anything *more* than a person were conceivable)—can hope to do justice to the Christian gospel.

Jesus' use of *Abba* and his proclamation of the coming of the kingdom probably should be seen in relation to each other. Turn them any way you will. God as the Eschatological One who is bringing the world under his reign is *Supernatural* Person; God as *Abba* is Supernatural *Person*. It is because we have found an *Abba*-type relationship to God that we are able to share his eschatological perspective toward the world. Christ's invitation for men to enter the kingdom, to participate in a new relationship of lordship toward the world, is simply the obverse side of his invitation for them to call God *Abba*, to participate in a new relation of sonship toward God himself.

Would that the new theology might teeter-totter these complementary emphases as well as Jesus himself did.

But what is probably the most fantastic movement ever attempted in responsible theology is that of the God-is-dead men who necessarily must excise from the Jesus-melody both the kingdom of *God* and God as *Abba* and yet presume to call the remaining notes (if there are any remaining) the song of Jesus.

CHAPTER SIX

THE MAN AND HIS DADDY

This little book—precisely that it might remain a *little* book —began with the firm resolve to discuss only the topic of God in his relation to man—nothing else, not Christology, ecclesiology, pistology, or any such. We have not done too well. It has become apparent that a Christian cannot talk about God and man without the talk drifting toward the Jesus who stands as the paradigm of such relationship. So we drift boldly.

The New Testament evidence is that "the Son of Man" is the one Christological title that Jesus himself recognized and adopted, although just how he used it and what he understood by it is still very much a matter of debate. The likelihood is that "the Son of Man" was an Aramaic idiom which more accurately could be expressed in English simply as "The Man." Although not knowing what he did, Kierkegaard was right in taking as a touchstone for his understanding of Jesus the centurion's verdict at the crucifixion, the verse which his Danish Bible misrendered as "Behold the man!"

"The Man" represents a deep, multifaceted crystal of thought which had been in formation through the ages, a product of the whole Eastern world. It stands behind Paul's discussion of the First Adam and the Second, the prototype man of the beginning who somehow is also the consummate man of the end, father of the race in the old creation and first-born of the new. According to the ancient concept, "The Man" both carries his own people with him in the present and in due course will incorporate humanity as his body. The idea also involves the royal enthronement myths that permeate the Old Testament tradition even as they antedate it. As he is enthroned, the king reiterates the drama of the one who, by obediently enduring humiliation, consequently is exalted to the dignity of "The Man," the man who has become, as first he was created, little less than God.[1]

"The Man" is a thought to conjure with—to conjure study

---

[1] The definitive study of this catena of tradition is Frederick Houk Borsch, *The Son of Man in Myth and History* (Philadelphia: Westminster Press, 1967).

about what it means to be man, about where humanity is headed and where it should be headed. And the conjuration continues today. Even the phrase "the man" is prominent in the vocabulary of blacks and teen-agers, where it points particularly to the guy who has "muscle," who can apply "crunch," the raw power and authority to impose his will upon others. "The man" is the object both of jealousy and fear. Jesus would qualify on some counts and fall dismally short on others.

And even where the phrase is not used, the conjuring continues. The mass media and advertising are obsessed with a search for "the man"—the man from Marlboro country, the Playboy, Cool Hand Luke—the image is kaleidoscopic while, strangely enough, it bores us with its sameness. There is no need to compound that boredom by trying a characterization of this man here; anyone capable of reading this book is capable of eliciting the image for himself.

"The man" of today does bear some resemblance to The Man Jesus; today's is an authentic quest for humanity. Yet he also is a perversion of the Jesus picture; Jesus' authority never took the form of muscle, to cite just one instance.

But perhaps the images are similar enough that we can bridge from one to the other. Could modern man be induced to transmute his "man" picture into a greater and greater likeness of The Man Jesus, would not this be his salvation?

91

Some such assumption seems to underlie most contemporary versions of the secular gospel, and the proposal even has been given the big try earlier. Classic liberalism was an attempt at such transmutation—although, as chance would have it, Jesus got transmuted more than "the man" of his liberal students did.

But it is no go; there is a rub that must give us pause. At one subtle but crucial point "The Man" and "the man" are antithetical (and here our teeter board begins to shift); there can be no bridge. *The Man had a Daddy.* The one who was original in taking to himself the title "Son of Man" ("The Man") is the very one who was original in addressing God as *Abba,* the smallest child's most intimate expression of utter dependence. Amazing, yea, impossible juxtaposition! Yet these two are notes most authentic and most basic to the melody of the historical Jesus.

Consider that the word *Abba* is absolutely the last a person ever could expect to hear spoken by today's "man." His hallmark is precisely the absence of a Daddy; he is, above all, self-sufficient, independent, his own determinator. According to modern thought, a Daddy relationship is the diametric opposite of manhood.

Clearly it was not so with Jesus. Rather it was his knowing God as *Abba* that made him "The Man." John's Gospel has Jesus saying what is obvious throughout all the Gospels: "I can do nothing on my own authority; as I hear, I judge; and my judgment is just, because I seek not my own will but the will of him who sent me. If I bear witness to myself, my testimony is not true. . . . Truly, truly, I say to you, the Son can do nothing of his own accord, but only what he sees the Father doing" (John 5:30-31, 19).

"Christianity is," as Kierkegaard once said, "the true humanism"; the Christ it proclaims is "The Man." But the secret of his manhood was that he called God *Abba*. These two elements cannot be separated; the evidence is clear that Jesus himself saw them as one piece. And thus it is impossible for natural man to make a natural transition from secular humanism to the true humanism of Christianity. The gospel is correct in portraying that transition as a death and resurrection, for one of the key assertions of that gospel is the very teetery-tottery proposition that true maturity is to know that one is but a child.

True maturity is to know that one is but a child!

CHAPTER SEVEN

FREE TO FLEE—
FREE TO FLY

If God is a person, he is free; our definition of "a person" prescribed that his acts demonstrate a certain freedom of decision and self-determination. By the same token, of course, every other person is free as well; and the problem of God's freedom in relation to man's is not intrinsically different from the problem of one man's freedom in relation to that of other men.

However, because God is a supernatural person who thus stands superior to nature rather than confined within it, his freedom takes on a qualitative distinction. Then, to call him the Lord of history—the one who not only stands above the natural world but who also directs it—pushes his freedom to an even higher pitch. And finally, to talk of his eschatological perspective implies that he already has used his freedom to determine the outcome of history as the playwright determines the outcome of his play. Where, in this setup, is there any room for the freedom of the rest of us persons? To put the matter bluntly, is the personhood of God, as we have described it, even compatible with the personhood of man? This problem becomes particularly acute when the new theology is intent, as it is, on stressing the freedom and ability of man. What can we say?

Perhaps an analogy can help. Think of a chess game in which one player is God the Master and the other, man, the rank amateur. In one sense (and a very real sense) the two players are equally free: each gets the same number of moves; the same rules apply to each. Nonetheless, the skill of the Master upsets that balance completely. The outcome of the game is effectively determined even before it starts—although not by abrogating the freedom of the greenhorn. One crucial distinction between the two players is that the Master operates out of what is precisely an eschatological perspective; it is not that the game is predetermined but that *his* game is *planned*. The Master has a consistent strategy and relates his every move to it; the amateur improvises as he goes along.

95

As the game proceeds, the Master moves so as to preserve his freedom of action, to keep his possibilities open and even to enhance them. The amateur throws his freedom away, giving up men unnecessarily, and finally working himself into a corner. Before long the Master actually has the amateur playing *his* game. And then the contest becomes eschatological in the strictest sense; the Master can say just where, when, and how the game will end. The Master has showed himself to be both lord and eschatological mover *without overstepping the freedom of the amateur at any point.* God does not have to deprive man of his freedom in order to accomplish his own holy purposes within history.[1]

Of course, the weakness of this analogy is that it pits man and God against each other when in reality this is but apparently the case; in fact the rule (kingdom) of God, his "winning," is synonymous with the fulfillment of man, his "winning." Man and God are working toward precisely the same goal, but the hardest thing in the world for man to do is to admit that only God knows where it is and how to get us there. Man would rather choose his own way and goal and then label it as "the kingdom of God"—it sounds so pious that way! Yet this is the very exegesis that the term "kingdom

---

[1] After this book was written someone pointed out that it was William James who had invented the chess game analogy—and I thought I had! I relinquish the honor but still claim credit for thinking James's thoughts after him.

(rule) *of God"* most emphatically disallows. The way for man to win is to let God win, and the way for man to be free is to let God be Lord. Human freedom, then, is a very teetery-tottery thing. The new theology hasn't realized that, but Grandfather Kierkegaard did:

"The most tremendous thing which has been granted to man is: the choice, freedom. And if you desire to save it and preserve it there is only one way: in the very same second unconditionally and in complete resignation to give it back to God, and yourself with it. If the sight of what is granted to you tempts you, and if you give way to the temptation and look with egoistic desire upon the freedom of choice, then you lose your freedom. And your punishment is: to go on in a kind of confusion priding yourself on having—freedom of choice, but woe upon you, that is your judgment: You have freedom of choice, you say, and still you have not chosen God." [2]

That may sound more like contradiction than dialectic, but it is not. Man is man and not God, and thus man's freedom must be of the order of the creature rather than the freedom of God himself. Man is free to choose whether or not he will fulfill his true destiny, but he is not free to choose what that destiny shall be.

[2] *The Journals of Kierkegaard,* trans. and ed. Alexander Dru (New York: Harper Torchbook Edition, 1959), p. 189.

97

Theoretically at least, any person is free to make of himself what he will (better, to *try* to make of himself what he will). But because his makeup does not qualify him equally for every role, to choose and commit himself to a role for which he is not fitted is effectively to abrogate his freedom. One hardly can be called free when he is in a situation he can't handle. So—again, theoretically at least—there must be one role (even down to such details as where I live, whom I marry, how many children I have) for which I am more suited than any other and in which I could operate more freely than in any other. This optimum role is what we call the will of God—or more precisely, at any given juncture the will of God is the choice which, under the prevailing circumstances, will move me closer to that role.

A person cannot be free in the truest sense until he knows who he is, cannot be free to play his melody until he knows what melody it is. And, as we quoted Kierkegaard earlier, "There is only One who knows what He Himself is, that is God; and He knows also what every man in himself is, for it is precisely by being before God that every man is. The man who is not before God is not himself." Inevitably then it follows, as Kierkegaard said above, that the only way a person can preserve his freedom is by giving it back to God—and himself with it.

What, then, is man's true destiny as man? And what is

Vernard Eller's true destiny as Vernard Eller? Only God knows, because only God has the eschatological perspective of the scriptwriter. The way, then, for man to get free and stay free is to let God tell him how.

Perhaps another analogy can help us here. It is the story of "The Grand Puppet-Master and His Living Marionette."

Once upon a time the Grand Puppet-Master—who had skill, ingenuity, and wisdom beyond description—created a "living" marionette, one entirely different and more marvelous than anything he had done before. In some respects it was a person as truly as was the Puppet-Master himself, but in other respects it was still clearly a marionette; it was built to operate at the hand of the Master, under the guidance and with the help of his strings. Nonetheless the marionette did have a real life of its own, with intelligence, will, and ability scaled to its miniature size and appropriate to its wood and plaster construction—yet truly alive for all that. Indeed, so much did the Puppet-Master respect this "livingness" that he vowed not to pick up the strings until the marionette asked him to.

(Because "puppets" are the last thing that modern men—and especially new theologians—are willing to be called, we need to be very specific about this "living marionette." It was *free* in the fullest respect possible within the limits of its nature and setting. In the first place, the Master would use the controls *only* when asked. But more, these controls were gossamer threads completely incapable of moving the marionette's limbs contrary to its own desires. The marionette was by no means devoid of either power or will; guidance and orientation was all that the Master proposed to provide. This hardly was a "puppet" in the usual sense of the term.)

When the marionette came alive (so to speak) it found itself on the workbench, its control stick hung on a nail overhead. The puppet, of course, had no way of knowing what it was supposed to be or how it was supposed to act. "Does one stand upon one's feet, one's hands, or one's head? And for that matter, which are hands, feet, and/or head?" It did some very clumsy experimenting without achieving much that could be called success. The uncoordinated threshing and inane posturing would have been laughable—if one happened not to think upon the smooth and beautiful performance for which the Puppet-Master had designed.

It was not long before the marionette discovered its sky-reaching strings and shortly after theorized, correctly enough, that they were controls. The only difficulty was that, looking from its puppet-centered perspective, it made a bad guess as to which end of the control was which. The marionette invented some interesting little patterns and ceremonies of string-pulling—which gave it a certain gratification in making the heavens shake but which accomplished not a whit toward discovering what it was supposed to be and do. What all this did accomplish, however, was to jog the control stick off the nail—and so produce a nasty clout on the head and a profound disillusionment with religion.

Continuing its fumbling efforts to find a role for itself, the marionette soon was rolled tight into a cocoon of string. Thereupon it reached the puppet-headed conclusion that the strings themselves were the source of all its trouble. "Get these religious fetters off me," it cried, "these strings that lead to nothing but a dead stick. I am of age and could take care of myself, were it not for these trammels of yesterday's superstition. I would be *free!"*

"You *are* free, little one, that is just your trouble. But have it as you will," the Puppet-Master responded as he bent to loose the strings one by one.

But the now newly freed marionette was more helpless than ever. It still had no notion of what it was created to be, and without the strings it even had lost its orientation as to which way was up. A marionette without strings is a pitiable sight.

Then finally, at long last the prodigal puppet came to itself. "I'm sorry," it cried. "I should have let you help me from the first. I am no longer fit to be called your living marionette; make me as one of your rag dolls. Make me a captive, Lord, and then I shall be free."

But before the words were out, the Puppet-Master was re-fastening the strings. And very shortly, when the control stick was in hand and the strings were taut, the marionette suddenly discovered what it had never dreamed before: he [not "it" now, but "he"] was a *dancer*. And dance he did! What fun! Running, jumping, pirouetting—as free as a bird!

"And now," the Puppet-Master laughed, "you know what it means to be free!"

The new theological emphasis upon the freedom, responsibility, capability, and high calling of man is very much in order. But what also needs to be emphasized is that it is only in relation to God, in sonship, that man finds these things. God's lordship, rightly seen, is the source and vehicle of man's freedom, not a threat to it. Seesawing gets to be fun only when there is a teeter for every totter.

We would do well here to take cognizance of what it is we have accomplished (or at least attempted) up to this point. Certainly ours has been an effort to clarify and elucidate, to make God more understandable. However, ours has *not* been the intention of making him more *acceptable*, easier to believe in. Our desire has been to come up with the truest possible understanding of the God of the biblical revelation, not to design a doctrine with an eye toward appealing to the sensibilities of modern man.

After all, the honest truth is that our claim that history itself shows forth the character of personal communication, of an identifiable individual seeking to encounter and establish dialogue with us human individuals (and even with *me*, a single human individual)—essentially this claim is just as fantastic as any dealing with a bearded old man in the sky. And when we talk about freedom being found in submission to a superior will—this hardly is an understanding of freedom that modern man will rush to embrace. And to suggest that the determination of the outcome of history is not ultimately a human option. . .

There are some hang-ups that modern man is going to have to get over for himself, which cannot be taken care of through theological adjustments. Jesus was pointing to something fundamental when he said, "Blessed is he who is not offended in me." Does not this warning compel us to recognize that essential to the Christian faith are some features which inevitably will be offensive to natural man (and which were just as offensive to men of the first century as to those of the twentieth); that to attempt to remove or defuse these is not to enhance the faith but to destroy it; and that blessedness comes not in evading these offenses but precisely in surmounting them?

CHAPTER EIGHT

RELIGIONLESSNESS— FOR GOD'S SAKE!

It was from the prison letters of Bonhoeffer that the concept of "religionlessness," or "religionless Christianity," took off to become a movement (or a fad?). The idea had been stated just as explicitly, although not as spectacularly, by Karl Barth. And there are beginnings of the concept (and even the terminology) clear back in Blumhardt. The heirloom had been in the family for three generations before its value generally was recognized.

However, particularly from Bonhoeffer and to a lesser degree from his forebears, what we get is a "tottered" version of religionlessness: that is, religionlessness is proposed for the sake of man, for the sake of man's fighting himself free from the fetters of "religion." Whether or not it reflects his deepest intention, Bonhoeffer almost proposed religionlessness for the sake of *twentieth-century man,* as though religion were right and proper for earlier Christians but not for the new breed of cat that is taking over today. This is tottered religionlessness, the clear effect of which is to celebrate the upswing of man.

Yet even though tottering is an appropriate movement of the seesaw, old Grandfather Kierkegaard had presented a "teetered" version of religionlessness way back when—although, unfortunately, he failed to use the terminology and so got his heirloom relegated to the cluttered attic of history. Nevertheless, we contend that religionlessness cannot be right until it is teeter-tottered and that even man's totter works better as a countermovement to God's prior teeter rather than vice versa. In any case, because this book is entitled *His End Up,* if for no other reason, we choose to go with Kierkegaard rather than Bonhoeffer—even though we have no real quarrel with Bonhoeffer at all.

To talk about religionlessness demands the prior step of defining the "religion" to which we propose to attach "-lessness." Obviously "religion" is here used in a "bad" sense, but the word itself resists such high-handed treatment. There must be retained a sense in which the word can be "good." Notice, for instance, that even the books that are most insistent on religionlessness are found in publishers' catalogs, in bookstores and libraries, under the heading "Religion"—and it could not properly be any other way. "Religion" in this broad sense denotes man in conscious relationship to God; and in this sense Bonhoeffer, Barth, Blumhardt, and Kierkegaard were deeply religious men and interested in helping us all become such.

But these men saw also that there is another sense in which "religion" must go if the God relationship is to have any chance of being true. The usage, then, presupposes two different modes of the God relationship: the religious mode, which is the defective one, and the faith mode, which is the true one. The difference between them is this: faith is an immediate, face-to-face relationship; religion is a controlled or mediated one. Consider that, in the face-to-face relationship which is the only possible situation for true dialogue, the cardinal principle is that each party leave the other free to speak his own piece in his own way at his own time. As soon as one person makes any attempt to influence or control the other end of the conversation as well as his own, true dialogue is all over. The faith relationship obtains, then, when God and man each leave the other free to be himself. God being who he is, there is not much danger of his trying to force man into anything (although, very obviously, some *men* do try to *use* God to force other men); but sad to say, men being who they are, their propensity is very much toward trying to force God into what they think he ought to be. "Religion," then, is the electronic instrumentation through which man tries to make God play.

Imagine for yourself such a spread; make it as big, as expensive, as sophisticated as you will; all of that lavish gadgetry exists for the sole purpose of giving the owner all possible control over what he is to hear. Central to the whole setup is the little on-off switch which enables him to choose *when* he is or is not going to listen. The channel selector or tuner gives him alternatives as to *what* he shall hear—the ultimate control in this regard being, I suppose, the turntable or tape deck. The volume, tone, stereo, and no telling what other controls let him determine *how* it shall sound. And if he wires a speaker system throughout the house, he even can determine *where* it shall play.

Just so, religious man sets up a lot of ecclesiastical gadgetry supposedly dedicated to the glory of God but actually lying very much within man's own control. Thus there are established holy places ("houses of God") where man can go to find God or stay away from to avoid God, as the mood may dictate. There are holy men who have officially approved ways of getting one through to God or obtaining for one favors from God. There are holy rites, rituals one can perform in order to make God's grace come. There are holy deeds—either wickednesses one can avoid or philanthropies one can support

107

—which are guaranteed to get one on the good side of God. There are holy beliefs which the creeds and confessions certify as being God's own understanding of himself. And there is a holy book, the letter of which can assure man that he holds a mortgage on God.

This is the religion that must go, although it does not automatically follow that all the outward structures and acts of the Christian life are forbidden. We should know that the stereo set is not the only use to which electronic gadgetry can be put; there is also the hearing aid. Consider that here also are microphones, speakers, transistors, and the like— used, however, not to give the owner control over the other who is the speaker, but directed toward his own deficiency precisely so that the other might have more freedom in his speaking, the freedom of being heard by the impaired ear. Thus the mere presence of electronics does not necessarily spell "religion"—although some setups are very obviously stereos rather than hearing aids; yet in the final analysis it is one's motivation and use of the gadgetry that determines whether it is the handmaiden of faith or the instrument of religion.

The point Kierkegaard stressed, however, is that the biblical-historical record of the faith makes it plain that God's most effective contacts with man have come in the absence of

108

religious gadgetry and, conversely, that the more the gadgetry, the harder it has been for God to get through.

Applying Kierkegaard's observation to the Bible, it becomes apparent that religionlessness is one of its most fundamental principles—revealed perhaps for the first time and most incisively in the crucial little exchange between God and Moses at the burning bush (Exodus 3:13-15). When God asked Moses to go way down in Egypt land and tell old Pharaoh, Moses responded that if he were to undertake a project of that magnitude he would *have* to know the name of God. Most scholars are agreed that the source of Moses' concern was a felt need for a name *by which God could be invoked.* What is the name that God will answer to, that will make him come, "Fido," "Spot," or what? Moses' interest was a "religious" one, pure and simple.

God's reply was that his name is Yahweh; this is formed from the Hebrew verb "to be," and the name therefore means "I am who I am" (or some such; there is a problem of translation). The customary interpretation until recently has been that God acceded to Moses' request and that the name is to be understood as carrying some sort of ontological affirmation about God being made out of pure "being" or some ether of that sort. However, latter-day scholars have determined that a Hebrew, and not Paul Tillich, wrote the Exodus account and

109

that it is inconceivable that a Hebrew God would be named after "being."

In light of this finding, the Jewish scholar Martin Buber has worked over the Hebrew text and the translation to propose that "I am who I am" actually was intended to mean "I will be present as I will be present." If Buber is right, then God has a most religionless name. It says in effect, "You don't need to invoke *me*; I'll be there; I'll be there before you get there. 'God on the Spot'—that's my name, and you need have no worries on that score. However, the fact that you have that promise does not give you any religious toehold on me, because I reserve the right to decide *how* I will be present. Sometimes I may be near to comfort and cheer, but sometimes it may be in order to place a well-aimed swat—that's for me to decide. So you don't need any religious gadgetry to make me come; I'm already there. And any gadgetry that tries to tell me what to do once I'm there just won't work." That, in a rough way, is how Buber reads Exodus 3.

The Jerusalem Bible, a Roman Catholic work, gets to the same place via a different route. It retains the wording "I am who I am" but interprets this as actually constituting God's refusal to give Moses his name. God is saying in effect, "My name is my business, and I can handle it. You worry about your name and let me worry about mine. Our whole relationship will be better off that way." The God of the burning bush is the God who refuses to let his name be turned to the advantage of man's religion.

But whichever reading is correct (or neither), it still is unimpeachable that, regardless of his name, God's character is precisely of this sort. Notice the points in the biblical story, the manner in which God most tellingly confronted man—the very opposite of what "religion" would expect or desire: through the prophets, uncredentialed free-lancers who were protesting and even attacking the religious establishment; in the actual destruction of the holy temple, the holy city, and the holy land—to the exiles in Babylon; through the birth of a peasant baby in a stinking cow barn—completely out of sight of the temple, priests, and all such; through the execution of the Savior and that as a condemned criminal—and with the religious establishment doing the condemning. How religionless can a God get?

In light of Kierkegaard's understanding of religionlessness as being the act by which man leaves God free to be God in his own way, it should become plain that "God is dead" is not a religionless move at all. Far from freeing God to be God, these theologians simply have used their stereo sets for the ultimate act of religion; they have turned them to "off" and then advanced this as proof that God speaks no more. Control over God has been made complete, and man has become free —or has he?

If the argument of our previous chapters is correct and God is the orientation point for an eschatological perspective toward the world, then man's freedom, far from consisting in an escape from God, must consist of a relationship toward him that is marked precisely by its allowing God to be God on his own terms. The absolute condition for man's becoming free is that he let the Beacon stand inviolate; and "religion"— through the very fact that it is an attempt to nudge that Beacon, to tell it when and where and how to shine—spells the end of man's freedom. Man can be free only if God is left free, and the freedom of God demands religionlessness on the part of man.

Thus both Bonhoeffer and Kierkegaard are right, but Kierkegaard the more so. Religionlessness promoted simply for the sake of man's freedom can be perverted into an escape from God and thus backfire as the *finis* of any true freedom. However, the religionlessness that is interested first and foremost in freeing God will guarantee the conditions for man's freedom at the same time. A free God is the precondition for free men. Religionlessness—for God's sake!

A word should be said at this point about "secular Christianity." This often has been used as synonymous with religionlessness, but to do so is to lose a distinction that can be of vital importance. In our argument at least, the dichotomy

112

"religion/religionlessness" is not at all the same thing as "sacred/secular." "The sacred" we understand as denoting that sphere of activity in which God consciously and publicly is recognized, in which his existence, presence, and relevance openly are affirmed. "The secular," conversely, is the sphere in which God's name is not named and in which his presence is for the most part ignored or at least recognized only in a desultory way. According to this definition, then, both of our previous categories, religion and religionlessness, fall within the sacred sphere: religionlessness is the proper mode of the sacred, religion the improper.

But what, then, should "secular Christianity" suggest? First let us consider some current interpretations which neither Bonhoeffer nor any of his predecessors could have intended or desired.

The weirdest of all is the one that would maintain the distinction between sacred and secular just as hard and fast as ever, simply reversing the evaluation of them. Through the use of a John Birch concept of "paradox" (one of Robert Welch's favorite principles is that the Communists undermine good Americans by speaking in such an amazingly clever way that their words communicate exactly the opposite of what they actually say), it is maintained that the place where God most truly is to be found and heard is among those who disdain his name, and the place where he is most unlikely to

be found is in the church. Godless men are the most godly;
novelists and playwrights who make no pretense of accepting
the gospel are the ones who are speaking it most clearly; and
the church is the last place one would go to find faith. The
fact that most of those taking this line are themselves func-
tionaries of the church and drawing their salaries therefrom
would suggest rather strongly that we are dealing with cases
of self-hatred. But in any case, this can't qualify even as a
"creative misuse" of Bonhoeffer; it is nothing but a parody of
him.

A less sensational but still unBonhoefferian interpretation
is that the gospel has obliterated the distinction between secular and sacred. In this instance, at least in theory, the secular is
not exalted above the sacred as being the primary arena of
God's activity. What is suggested is that, as far as his getting
through to men and affecting their lives, it is all one to God
whether those men acknowledge his presence or not. God
can make himself heard as well by those who ignore his existence as by those who affirm it. Whereas in the previous instance the church was an unmitigated evil that kept men from
finding the God that secular men find, here it is simply useless, beside the point one way or the other. But we do not
have to follow this logic very far to see that it would also render
useless any proclamation of the gospel, any naming of God and
his Christ, any reading of the Bible. If God can get through

just as well without these things, then why bother? It is no more possible to reconcile this interpretation with Bonhoeffer's theological premises than we could the other one.

But even granting that the church has deeply corrupted herself with religion and is doing a very poor job of witnessing to her Lord, it is not necessary to go this other step to suggest that God would be as well off with no church at all or that he would be as well heard if men paid him no attention at all. No, the only view that will begin to do justice to the integrity of Bonhoeffer is the one that sees "secular Christianity" as the breakdown of the high, tight barrier that had separated the sacred from the secular, as the making of their border much more subtle, flexible, and open than it has been heretofore.

The distinction between sacred and secular is valid and will remain important, but the two spheres no longer can be maintained in isolation from each other. Several considerations are involved. For one thing, the sacred cannot now be understood simply as the domain and fief of the institutional church; the fact is that God is heard, acknowledged, named, and heeded quite beyond the reach of the church's permission and oversight. The sphere of the sacred takes in considerably more territory than simply the sphere of the organized church.

For another thing, following up our previous discussion of religionlessness, man dare not dictate that God confine his activity to the realm of the sacred. God can and may choose to break through to men who do not know or have never called upon his name, and Christians had better keep themselves open to that possibility—although it does not follow that the secular thereby becomes the most likely arena of God's activity.

Our earlier analogy of God as a melody is pertinent here. Theoretically, once a sound wave has been sounded it continues to reverberate omnipresently and eternally. And theoretically, too, the strains of "Three Blind Mice" go out through all the earth, and its words to the end of the world. But practically, with God as with sound waves, things do not work out quite that way: the closer one can get to the sound source, the clearer and more distinct the melody will be heard; the farther away one gets, the less the chance that he will hear it. And the Christian faith and testimony is that the primary sound source of "Three Blind Mice" lies in the salvation history of the Judeo-Christian tradition, preeminently in the life and career of Jesus of Nazareth, and in the records which we know as holy scripture. It stands to reason, then, that although it is possible for the melody to be heard deep within the realm of the secular, the chances of such hearing are much better within the realm of the sacred where "Three Blind Mice" is a recognized tune and where conscious attention is paid to Jesus and the Bible—and perhaps even better yet within the

116

smaller realm of the institutional church where organized community efforts at listening are conducted.

Finally, "secular Christianity" suggests that the isolation of the spheres is further broken down as the sacred proceeds to make its witness and take its servant role right out in the midst of secular life. The distinction between sacred and secular is not glossed over nor obliterated, but a spatial interpenetration does take place.

Yet, in another sense, one of the most basic premises of Christian eschatological perspective is precisely that an obliteration *is* in process—but one directly contrary to what the term "secular Christianity" might suggest and what much of the new theology supports. The biblical contention is that all of life is becoming *sacralized* (not secularized), pointing toward the day when "at the name of Jesus every knee shall bow, in heaven and on earth and under the earth, and every tongue confess that Jesus Christ is Lord, to the glory of God the Father." It is the secular sphere that is headed for obliteration, and not the sacred.

We will argue that along with the new theology's talk about secularization there needs to be talk about *sacralization;* the current emphasis is not as helpful as it could be, because it has not been treated dialectically, has not been teeter-tottered. We are not arguing against the "totter" of secularization; we do propose to introduce the "teeter" of sacralization.

Bonhoeffer, Harvey Cox, and others have been absolutely correct in spotting the biblical theme of secularization. Both the Old and the New Testaments are concerned to put the creation in its place; nothing in the world—not nature, not technology, not any ideology, not any state or government, not any "religion"—shall claim sacred status and so presume to tyrannize men. All shall be desacralized *so that God alone is God and Lord.* "There is none holy like the Lord, there is none besides thee; there is no rock like our God." (I Samuel 2:2.) Man is to lay low all his idols so that the true God can stand high; and to the extent that some of the new theologians imply that all things (including God) are to be laid low so that the iconoclast himself can stand high, this is to misunderstand biblical secularization totally.

But even biblical secularization is only half the story. Martin Buber, who understood the secularization theme as profoundly as Bonhoeffer or anyone else, saw that although the "holiness" of Yahweh does imply the secularizing of the whole creation, it also carries another implication of equal importance: " 'Holy' means distinct but not severed, distinct and yet in the midst of the people, distinct and radiating. . . . Yahweh is absolute master of the world because, although he is definitely distinct from the world, he is not in any way withdrawn from it. And for this very reason this conception makes possible a new and the highest expression of the demand to imitate God: that

118

Israel should be holy, as their God is holy. . . . Indeed Israel must—this is the meaning—be distinct, but not in order to withdraw itself from the world of nations, but in order to influence them by the radiance of its way of life. . . . Yahweh is present to Israel even with his most sublime and essential characteristic, his holiness, and . . . Israel is thereby able to receive his influence to follow his footsteps and to place human activity at the disposal of his activity." [1] This economy Buber calls "the *hallowing* of Israel by the *holy* Yahweh," a "sacralization" pure and simple—although not one that in any way contradicts the earlier movement of "secularization." Man's life must be secularized precisely in order that, as *secular* life, it might be sacralized for God.

But, please note, under our interpretation, "sacralization" carries *no* implications of otherworldliness. A major burden of this book has been to show that the Christian understanding of God, eschatological perspective, and everything else is very much *this*-worldly; we expressly have denied the necessity of positing another world. Yet if we accept the implicit assumption of much of the new theology, that *any* talk about God is perforce otherworldly, then we are in for big trouble. Let there be, indeed, a moratorium (nay, a final end) to otherworldly

[1] Martin Buber, *The Prophetic Faith* (New York: Harper Torchbook Edition, 1949), pp. 128-29.

119

talk about God, but let it not be suggested that this is to pro-hibit God-talk altogether.

Similarly, our definition of sacralization carries *no* "religious" implications. Let there be, indeed, a moratorium (nay, a final end) to all religious talk about God, i.e. talk which suggests that God can be channeled and used for our own purposes and convenience; but let it not be suggested that religiously is the only way God can be named. "Secularization-sacralization" is the truly Christian economy, and God hasten the day when every tongue shall confess—although, of course, God's name must be confessed in truth and not as a shibboleth of other-worldliness or religion. But to let our distaste for misuse of the name outlaw its proper usage is to jump from the frying pan into the fire, for the stickler that our secularist theologians simply have not been able to answer is how the good news that God so loved the world that he gave his only Son can be com-municated by one who refuses to name either God or his Son.

We would hold, however, that our definition of sacraliza-tion is in line with Bonhoeffer's "secular Christianity" and that what he intended was a Christianity committed to a sacralizing of the secular, not to a secularizing of the faith itself. Indeed, anything that could be called an "eschatological perspective" (and Bonhoeffer had a strong one) as much as demands a concept of sacralization, for what is the kingdom of God ex-cept *the creation sacralized?*

It often is overlooked that right in the midst of Bonhoeffer's letters discussing "secular Christianity" is one which pleads that God must be the *cantus firmus,* the ground bass, the sacralization(?), of one's life in the world. Further, in the outline of the book on religionlessness and secular Christianity which he did not get to write, he specifies that the church "must tell men, whatever their calling, what it means to live in Christ, to exist for others," and that the goal of our relation to God is "a new life for others, through participation in the Being of God." I personally would have preferred that he had said "*activity* of God," and the total context of his work would indicate that this is what he intends by "being." But in any case, a movement toward living in Christ and participating in the activity of God certainly would qualify as sacralization.

Here, then, is a naming of God which has driven so profound and deep that it may not be as blatant and obtrusive as the usual religious and otherworldly blather, but this hardly can be identified as a secularization that proposes either to de-emphasize or to quit naming God.

Name God? Of course; but take care to do it in spirit and in truth so that it is the true God who is named. "Secular Christianity"? Indeed so—if Bonhoeffer gets to define his term!

CHAPTER NINE

SOME TIMELY THOUGHTS
ON ETERNITY

It is in personal relationship to God as *Abba* that God as Lord becomes the orientation point by which one gets an eschatological perspective on the world. If God is to serve such orienting function, it is prerequisite that he be free to be God in his own way. And for God to be free demands that man be religionless. But what precisely, it must be asked, does this eschatological perspective do for a person? If it is merely a case of satisfying an apocalyptic curiosity about what maybe is going to happen one sweet day, then most people will be but little interested. What does it give us for the here and now? That is where modern man becomes interested.

Earlier we took pains to deny that the eschatological gospel of the New Testament seriously attempts (or even has any desire) to give us new and esoteric information about events of the hidden future. This, then, is not included in our concept of eschatological perspective. However, we also did maintain earlier that the gospel does offer some insights about the general character of history's coming denouement; and these, of course, can be of truly present help in enabling a person to align his own activity and efforts with the goal toward which history itself is moving.

But the matter can and must be made much more specific than this, because New Testament eschatology also carries with it another dimension. It consists not simply of insights regarding a future end but is also the announcement that, in Jesus Christ, that end even now is beginning to realize itself within the living present. Thus, to align oneself and gear in with the kingdom of God (for which the gospel offers not only the requisite know-how but the requisite invitation and enabling power as well) is not simply to get ready for something future but to get with a world which itself is in process of being readied for that future. Although the bare word "eschatology" may be a little misleading on this score, Christian eschatology has a very strong orientation toward the living present, for its basic premise is that the truest understanding of the present is to see it as the future in process of be-coming.

All this is tremendously significant, but that significance can be made even more pointed and practical. What eschatological perspective does for a person is to make it possible for him to distinguish between the actual and the real.

Our "actual/real" terminology will take a little explaining, but let us first say something about where it comes from. The idea, though not the terminology, comes from Kierkegaard. This in itself is something strange, that a basic aspect of eschatological understanding should come from a thinker who is seemingly as oblivious to eschatology as was Soren Kierke-gaard; he gave virtually no attention to the kingdom of God, the culmination of history, and such things. In that regard, it is one of the "too bad" passings in the dark of historical circumstance that Kierkegaard, the Lutheran layman of Copen-hagen, Denmark, did not get to know Blumhardt, the Lutheran pastor of Mottlingen, Germany. (On June 1, 1842, the day the younger Blumhardt was born, his father was involved in "the fight" with demonic powers which launched his career as a Christian leader, and Kierkegaard was writing *Either/Or*, the book which launched his literary career.) It is not as though Kierkegaard's thought were in any way anti-eschatological; and he might have been able to put Blumhardt's insights to very good use indeed. As it is, we will have to try to do for

124

the two men what the finitudes of this life kept them from doing for each other.

Be that as it may, the noneschatological Kierkegaard talked early and late about time and eternity, about eternity (or the eternal) breaking into time, about there being communication and contact between the two, and so on. However, what he understood or intended by "time" and "eternity" is a knotty little question, because it is obvious that the customary definitions will not apply. It is clear that "the eternal" and even "eternity" are almost synonymous with God himself, or at least with the activity of God; in many cases such a substitution would not change Kierkegaard's thought in the least. It also is clear that eternity does not denote a timeless world either hanging outside or concealed within our own or a quality of "being" underlying the "beings" of this world; such spatial and ontological thinking is completely foreign to him. And finally, eternity cannot be simply a future period that will succeed the present one; he speaks too often of their coincidence.

No, the alternative that promises to make Kierkegaard's terminology come clear is that time is existence as seen by man, by man in the middle. Eternity, on the other hand, is the same existence as seen by God, as seen in terms of what it is becoming (and "becoming" is undeniably one of Kierkegaard's central concepts, while his big word "existence" means precisely "that which is in process"), as seen from God's eschatological perspective. Kierkegaard's thought may include much more of the eschatological than anyone (including Kierkegaard) has guessed. In any case, by coming at it explicitly through eschatology, we will use "actual/real" in an attempt to explicate Kierkegaard's rather obscure "time/eternity."

The *actual,* then, is this world, human existence, as it can be and is empirically observed and analyzed from the standpoint of those who are on the spot. The assumption lying behind the *actual* view of things is that what thus can be observed is the final reality of that which is; things are what empirical analysis tells us they are and have no other sort of reality.

The *real,* on the other hand, marks the view which maintains that the *actuality* of what can be observed is only half the story; the *reality* of the thing includes the "shall be" which it is in process of becoming. We must be very careful at this point not to slip into a Platonic ontology that sees reality residing in an other-where world of ideal forms; our concept has nothing in common with that.

What we mean by "the *real*" is necessarily premised upon the faith that there is a God person who is the eschatological Creator, Lord, and Goal of the universe and of every person in it. In such case, the "shall be" which any thing or person is in process of becoming is much more fundamental, concrete, and real(?) than simply a possibility which he (it) may or may not choose to realize someday. No, the *real,* which shall be and which at present is coming to be, is also that which God in his intention chose it to be, that which he created it as being, that which he even now is working to make of it, and that which he shall eventually bring it through to be in all actuality. Although we are not used to thinking of the reality of a thing in these terms, it should be obvious that what is seen in this view is truly more fundamental and profound than is the simple actuality of the moment.

Notice that this *real* view makes no extrascientific claims about having perceived any sort of superempirical "being" or hidden dimensions within the observable actuality. No, reality is concerned with the very same object that actuality is, the difference being merely (*merely,* he says!) one of perspective. Actuality sees only that which is present in the moment and assumes that this is the thing in its reality; reality sees from the total eschatological perspective of the thing's origin, purpose, and destiny.

That which the real view makes possible but which is forever forbidden to the actual view is the distinction between sickness and health. Indeed, sickness, even in the most literal physiological sense, is simply a measure of the distance between actuality and reality. Consider that an M.D. can be of little help to anyone until he has a rather clear picture of the patient's *reality* as well as his *actuality*. For instance, if he tries to treat a fellow's dark skin condition without realizing that the man is a Negro, he has failed to take into account the reality of that man's skin, has assumed a discrepancy between actuality and reality which in this case does not exist. But conversely, if he fails to treat the next patient's broken nose because he misheard the name as "Durante," he has pulled the same boo-boo in reverse; he has seen the actuality of the nose and mistakenly assumed that it is the reality.

The analogy can be made even more pointed. A patient comes in with a forearm bent at a crazy angle (we should not have used that word "crazy," because it already implies a distinction between the actuality of what the arm is at the moment and the reality of what true arms are). Well, then, the patient comes in with a bent forearm. The doctor must know with some precision how that arm *really* is (i.e. how it was created to be, how it was, and how it should be) if he is to know whether the *actual* arm is discrepant from the norm and if he is to prescribe how to get that actuality again coincident with the arm's reality. And notice a most important aspect of the case: the *actuality* of the arm can be assessed simply through here-and-now observations of the present; the *reality* can be assessed only from an overarching perspective that encompasses something of the past and future as well as the present.

128

Now modern man, precisely because he has come of age, has become very sharp at making empirical analyses of the actual. He has invented x-ray machines for observing forearms, electron microscopes for observing teeny-weenies, telescopes for observing the stars, and opinion polls for observing the social animal. There is no denying that he is real good at making observations. So, too, he is gaining some impressive ability in manipulating that which he observes. He may not yet be able to manipulate with quite the finesse with which he observes—but he is getting there and rapidly. Perhaps man's progress in these areas accurately can be described as an outgrowing of a need for God.

But notice that these skills concern only the *actual* and do not even touch the concept of the *real*. Even man come of age is still very much man in the middle—man just as irrevocably confined to the middle as any of his forefathers were. Modern man's newfound powers over the actuality of the present do not imply the slightest achievement of a new perspective which would provide either an insight into understanding or ability in approaching the reality of the universe, grounded as that is in the mind and intentions of God. Eschatological perspective, the ability to discern reality, can come only as a gift from God; and nothing man can do (whether he is of age or not) ever will change that situation or obviate that need for help.

However, it should be noted, the obverse is hardly the case. Man's coming of age has not changed his need for eschatological perspective, but if he were willing to let God provide him with that perspective, then the fact that he has come of age would be very much to the point. His powers of observing and manipulating the actual present could be directed toward and aligned with the overall eschatological movement toward the kingdom of God. In such case, the world would see the awe-inspiring fulfillment of Jesus' prediction that we shall do "greater things than these"——although the fact that we presently are doing some pretty *big* things is no evidence that they are *great* in any sense that Jesus would recognize.

But the sad truth is that modern man by and large is *not* going to go to God for eschatological perspective. The admission that man needs God in order to be man is not one that a coming-of-age adolescent is about to make. The alternative then (and the one to which modern man already is as good as committed) is to make the simple assumption that "the actual" *is* "the real"——a simple assumption indeed, but a very dangerous one also.

In this situation the unfortunate weakness of the new theology is that, through its failure to give God the dialectical upswings he deserves, it effectively has gone along with modern man in assuming the coincidence of the actual and the real. But now when the new theology talks as it does about becoming "realistic," it is using the wrong word; the new theology is "actualistic"; without God there is no eschatological perspective, and without eschatological perspective there is no way of becoming "realistic."

How this *quid pro quo* works out in practice is rather easy to see. The new theology assumes that today's actual men—the modern men of whom, to whom, and for whom it speaks—are real men. And thus, rather than dealing with the understanding of the real God that *real* men would hold, its tendency is to adjust the gospel to conform to what *actual* men are willing to accept. The case is as if the doctor, mistakenly assuming that his patient is healthy (has "come of age" in the unBonhoefferian sense of the term), tells him to eat what he wants—when the fact of the matter is that the man's sick appetite simply will feed his sickness.

The situation is perhaps even more apparent as regards the new theology's morality department. The New Testament presented an impossibly high moral code—a code, we better would say, that was impossibly high for *actual* men (and as much so then as now). But speaking more profoundly, this New Testament ethic was not a code then and never was intended to be such; it was a *description*, written from an eschatological perspective, portraying the character and style of *real* men, and so intended to challenge and help *actual* men in their growth toward the reality of the kingdom. Indeed, the

131

disparity between the picture of today's *actual* men and the New Testament's picture of *real* men is a striking indication of how sick we truly are.

Now the new morality has become aware of the disparity but, under the assumption that *actual* modern man is for *real*, has had to brand the New Testament ethic as unrealistic (of all things!). And thus the tendency has been to scale down that ethic to make it conform to the context in which men *actually* live. But in effect this comes to be a morality which, at best, can help preserve man in his sickness (having, of course, assumed that that sickness is health), perhaps keeping him from becoming any sicker but certainly not giving him any vision or help toward becoming what he could be and *really* is.

At this point it becomes apparent how utterly self-defeating it is for theology to try to enhance the upswings of man by de-emphasizing those of God. By failing to teeter, the new theology, at best, can glorify only *actual* man; but give God his turn and, lo and behold, the next end to come up carries on it *real man,* the man God created as his partner on the seesaw.

Just how this can work out to the glorification of both has been no better presented than by the younger Blumhardt, and nowhere do we find a better example of what eschatological perspective can do:

"When God created the world he founded his kingdom on

132

earth. The earth was his kingdom. And who was to reign, to rule, and to watch over it as his representative? *Man.* God's kingdom was in paradise through man. One true man—and God's kingdom is here! An Adam, and there it was, God himself in paradise. A man was there, and God was with this man. Nothing else was of any importance.

"The loss of man was the world's catastrophe. Man was gone. True man was missing. False men with a false spirit, with false desires and false aims, think they are real men. Yet they are unhappy, because in reality they are false men. The false man is the world's undoing. True man is still missing and will be missing until Jesus comes and does away with the false man. Yet now we do have the fortune to know that there is one in whom the world is God's again, in whom all that is created is again placed into the light of the first creation. This one is Jesus, the Son of Man, more real than any other man, more childlike than all other children. He lives among men, and he *is* the kingdom of God." [1]

---

[1] *Christoph Blumhardt and His Message,* ed. R. Lejeune (Rifton, N.Y.: Plough Publishing House, 1963), pp. 158 and 160. I have taken the liberty of excerpting and rearranging Blumhardt's sentences in order to present his thought in a more logical and condensed form.

CHAPTER TEN

ESV: TIME TRIP TOWARD TOTALITY
An Essay in Theological Fiction

This chapter marks a "first"—certainly not the first time that theological fiction has been written but the first time a writer willingly has labeled his stuff as such. However, the label should not be understood as self-derogation. Science fiction is a perfectly respectable genre (better, science fiction *can* be respectable), and theology—particularly if it intends to operate out of an eschatological perspective—could do with the same sort of adjunct.

Science fiction is the attempt, on the basis of present scientific knowledge, to project the future which the course of

134

science may bring about. Actually it is a pretty miserable sort of eschatology, because, at most, it can represent only a projection made by a man stuck fast in the middle and not a communication with the God who enjoys a truly eschatological perspective. But if theology does have access to such a perspective, then it ought to be busy picturing for us what real, future man is going to look like, what the real, future world is going to look like—in short, what the on-its-way kingdom of God and its citizens are going to look like. Such picturing, unlike science fiction, would not be simply for entertainment; it is essential to the cause of theology (and the cause of man).

Recently, somewhere in the Midwest a professional planning expert (whether industrial, civic, or whatever, I do not know) addressed an audience on how to pursue projects most effectively. The major thrust of his speech was that every step of planning and building must be done in terms of one's "end-state vision." Now there is a term that theology can use; in fact, theology should have come up with it first. End-state vision (ESV) certainly is the key for theological fiction and should be the focus of the entire theological enterprise. So take a dose of ESV, close your eyes, and prepare for the "trip"—time trip toward totality.

Coming toward us is a man of the end-state. His character is immediately obvious, marked by such attributes as love, joy, peace, patience, kindness, goodness, faithfulness, gentleness, self-control; against such there is no law. He supplements his faith with virtue, and virtue with knowledge, and knowledge with self-control and self-control with steadfastness, and steadfastness with godliness, and godliness with brotherly affection, and brotherly affection with love. . . .

Publisher's Note: Apparently this will have to stand as it is, the world's first, shortest, and last essay at theological fiction. The author's manuscript breaks off at this point, undoubtedly from the sudden realization that his whole book was in danger of being exposed as old hat if not outright fraud: this theological fiction bit had been done somewhere before. And what is worse, none of it is "fiction" in any sense of the term. There are current a number of reliable reports that some time ago now one such end-state man actually lived among us. He went under the name Jesus.

However, because the author was not man enough to finish what he started, we have called upon his great-grandfather Kierkegaard to write an appropriate conclusion. It will become obvious in the following that Kierkegaard utterly fails to point out that the end-state vision which the royal coachman brings to the situation is nothing more nor less than the actual/real distinction of eschatological perspective. But this can be forgiven; after all, Kierkegaard had to write the conclusion one hundred and seventeen years before the book was written.

CONCLUSION
by S. Kierkegaard

Once upon a time there was a rich man who brought from abroad, at an exorbitant price, a team of faultless and excellent horses which he wanted for his own pleasure and the pleasure of driving them himself.

A year or two passed by. If anyone who had known these horses in earlier days now saw them driven by their owner, he would not be able to recognize them. Their eyes had become dull and drowsy; their pace had no carriage and consistency. They could bear nothing; they could endure nothing. The rich man could hardly drive them four miles without having to stop on the way, and sometimes they came to a standstill just when he was driving his best. Moreover, they had acquired all sorts of quirks and bad habits. Although they of course got food in abundance, they grew thinner day by day.

The rich man called in the king's coachman. He drove them for one month. At the end of the period there was no team of horses in the whole land which carried their heads so proudly, whose eyes were so fiery, whose pace was so beautiful. No other team of horses could hold out as they did, running even thirty miles in a stretch without stopping. How did this happen? It is easy to understand. The owner, who was no coachman and merely played the coachman, drove the horses according to the horses' conception of how they should be driven. The royal coachman drove them according to a coachman's conception of driving.

This is a picture of human life. When I think of myself and the countless people I have learned to know, I have often said to myself in sadness: "Here are capacities and powers and possibilities enough—but the driver is lacking." Through the long ages, for generation after generation, we human beings have been driven, if I may say so, according to the horses' conception of driving. We have been governed, trained, and educated according to man's conception of what it is to be a man. You see what has come from that—we lack spiritual stature. It follows from this again that we can endure so little, that we impatiently use the means of the moment, impatiently want to see instantaneous rewards for our labors, which for this very reason become of secondary importance.

Once it was otherwise. There was a time when it pleased the Deity Himself, if I may say so, to be the coachman, and He drove the horses according to a coachman's conception of what driving is. What was man not capable of then! . . .

No man has ever lifted his head so proudly in elevation over the world as did the first Christians in humility before God! As that team of horses could run on thirty miles without stopping to pant, so did they also run—ran seventy years in a

138

stretch without getting out of the harness, without pausing any place. Not proudly—for they were humble before God. They said, "It is not for us to lie down or loiter along the way. We make our first stop—in eternity!" It was Christianity which was to be carried through, and they carried it through, indeed they did! But they were also well-driven, indeed they were! [1]

[1] *For Self-Examination,* trans. Edna and Howard Hong, pp. 101-4. Used by permission of Augsburg Publishing House, Minneapolis, Minnesota, copyright owner. Copyright 1940 and 1968.

INDEX

142